A School Privatization Primer
for Michigan School Officials, Media and Residents

Mackinac Center for Public Policy

Michael D. LaFaive

A School Privatization Primer
for Michigan School Officials, Media and Residents
2007

Michael D. LaFaive

Guarantee of Quality Scholarship

The Mackinac Center for Public Policy is committed to delivering the highest quality and most reliable research on Michigan issues. The Center guarantees that all original factual data are true and correct and that information attributed to other sources is accurately represented.

The Center encourages rigorous critique of its research. If the accuracy of any material fact or reference to an independent source is questioned and brought to the Center's attention with supporting evidence, the Center will respond in writing. If an error exists, it will be noted in an errata sheet that will accompany all subsequent distribution of the publication, which constitutes the complete and final remedy under this guarantee.

ISBN-13: 978-1-890624-63-7
ISBN-10: 1-890624-63-2
S2007-07

About the Mackinac Center

The Mackinac Center for Public Policy is a nonpartisan research and educational institute devoted to improving the quality of life for all Michigan residents by promoting sound solutions to state and local policy questions. The Mackinac Center assists policymakers, scholars, business people, the media and the public by providing objective analysis of Michigan issues. The goal of all Center reports, commentaries and educational programs is to equip Michigan residents and other decision-makers to better evaluate policy options. The Mackinac Center for Public Policy is broadening the debate on issues that have for many years been dominated by the belief that government intervention should be the standard solution. Center publications and programs, in contrast, offer an integrated and comprehensive approach that considers:

All Institutions. The Center examines the important role of voluntary associations, communities, businesses and families, as well as government.

All People. Mackinac Center research recognizes the diversity of Michigan residents and treats them as individuals with unique backgrounds, circumstances and goals.

All Disciplines. Center research incorporates the best understanding of economics, science, law, psychology, history and morality, moving beyond mechanical cost-benefit analysis.

All Times. Center research evaluates long-term consequences, not simply short-term impact.

Committed to its independence, the Mackinac Center for Public Policy neither seeks nor accepts any government funding. The Center enjoys the support of foundations, individuals and businesses that share a concern for Michigan's future and recognize the important role of sound ideas. The Center is a nonprofit, tax-exempt organization under Section 501(c)(3) of the Internal Revenue Code. For more information on programs and publications of the Mackinac Center for Public Policy, please contact us.

140 West Main Street, P.O. Box 568, Midland, Mich. 48640; 989-631-0900, Fax 989-631-0964; www.mackinac.org • mcpp@mackinac.org

Contents

Acknowledgements

I would like to thank those who assisted in the research and preparation of this primer:

- James M. Hohman, Research Assistant, Mackinac Center for Public Policy;
- Thomas W. Washburne, Director of Labor Policy, Mackinac Center for Public Policy;
- Patrick J. Wright, Senior Legal Analyst, Mackinac Center for Public Policy;
- Daniel Himebaugh, Research Fellow, Reason Foundation;
- Matthew Piccolo, Research Fellow, Reason Foundation;
- Lisa Snell, Director of Education and Child Welfare, Reason Foundation;
- Geoff Segal, Director of Government Reform, Reason Foundation;
- Jim Palm, Assistant Superintendent, Berrien County Intermediate School District;
- Kenneth May, Principal of South Plainfield High School in New Jersey;
- Steve Hirano, Associate Publisher, School Bus Fleet;
- Robin Leeds, National School Transportation Association Industry Specialist;
- John Markey, Vice President/CEO, Absolute Building Maintenance;
- Rick Simpson, Regional Sales Director, Chartwells School Dining;
- Hannah K. Mead, Communications Intern, Mackinac Center for Public Policy.

This primer reflects their invaluable insights and generous assistance. I remain solely responsible for any errors that may remain.

An Overview
of Privatization

The word "privatization" has been part of the international lexicon since 1969, when management expert Peter Drucker used the term "reprivatization" in his book "The Age of Discontinuity."[1] Robert Poole of the Reason Foundation, a Los Angeles-based research institute, was primarily responsible for popularizing the concept in the 1980s.

There are varying degrees and types of privatization. In its most general sense, privatization involves an increased private-sector role in the management of government assets or the provision of government services. Examples include the sale of government assets to private owners; private management of government assets under a contract with a private asset manager; private management of government services and service employees; and private production of government-mandated services through contracts with private vendors.

Outside of the United States, privatization has long meant the sale of state-owned enterprises, such as airlines, railroads or ports. Within the United States, such sales have been infrequent, since this country was never as deeply involved in owning and running industries as other countries were. Nevertheless, the U.S. government has sold a few of its assets, most notably the Elk Hills Naval Petroleum Reserve, which generated $3.65 billion in new revenue.[2]

The more common form of federal government privatization involves contracting with private firms for public services formerly provided by federal employees. Some of these services are significant. For instance, the Pentagon is employing contractors in the U.S. war in Iraq and may privatize the military mail system.[3] The actual price for delivering military mail has been estimated at more than $1.8 billion annually, and a government task force concluded that contracting for this service could save 30 percent.[4]

Outside the Pentagon, the 2001 "President's Management Agenda" requires competitive bidding between private vendors and certain public agencies for services ranging from printing to fisheries management.[5] According to the Reason Foundation, 181 of these "competitions" between federal employees and private contractors took place in fiscal 2005. The competitions are expected to generate $3.1 billion in savings and cost avoidance over five to 10 years.[6]

Privatization at the state level is commonplace today, and the examples of privatization are as varied as the 50 states themselves. For example,

Michigan sold its worker compensation insurance business for more than $255 million in June 1994 — the largest single state asset sale in the nation's history at the time.[7] In New Mexico, more than 43 percent of state prison inmates are housed under contract with a private management company, according to the U.S. Bureau of Justice Statistics.[8]

Privatization is also common in counties, townships, cities and villages. Some localities have sold off city-owned parking garages and golf courses or contracted the management of such services as refuse collection, wastewater treatment, building permit inspections and rodent control. New York City has contracted with a nonprofit organization to manage the world-famous Central Park.[9]

Another area of government that has gained a great deal of experience in competitive contracting — especially in New Jersey, Rhode Island and Michigan — is public education. The privatization of major school support services — food, busing and janitorial — is the focus of this guide.

Public Education Spending and Personnel

Nationwide, public education is a vast undertaking. Total state and local revenues for public elementary and secondary education in fiscal 2005 were more than $443 billion.[10] To put this figure in perspective, in fiscal 2005 U.S. military spending was $483 billion, according to the Office of the U.S. Assistant Secretary of Defense for Public Affairs.[11] This military spending encompassed wars in Iraq and Afghanistan, $75.6 billion for the "Global War on Terror" and another $3.2 billion for disaster relief spending.[12]

Professor John Donahue of Harvard's Kennedy School of Government notes that America's public education system is so big that public school teachers make up the largest single group of government employees in the nation, with teachers' aides ranking second.[13] Despite the number of teachers and aides, however, a significant percentage of public school employees are not involved in instruction.

Citing the U.S. Bureau of Labor Statistics in his forthcoming book "The Warping of Government Work," Donahue reports that in 2002, there were 3.1 million nonteaching personnel employed in public education.[14] Some of these were involved with higher education, but Donahue calculates that around 2.3 million are nonteaching elementary and secondary public school employees.[15] Positions run the gamut from accountants, secretaries and counselors to bus drivers, janitors and cafeteria workers. In Michigan, data from the state's Center for Educational Performance and Information indicate that teachers, teachers' aides and instructional coordinators comprise 53 percent of Michigan's public education employees, while the remaining 47 percent of employees perform support work, including administration.[16]

Contracting of School Support Services

Many Michigan school districts face declining student enrollment. Between fiscal 2007 and fiscal 2008, state budget officials recently projected a loss of 15,575 students statewide, a decline of 0.93 percent.[17] Since the primary mechanism for financing operating expenditures in Michigan's elementary and secondary schools is the per-pupil foundation allowance, fewer students usually means fewer dollars. In addition, the rate of increase in the state's basic foundation allowance has declined somewhat in recent years.[i]

State school finance trends and the high number of school support service workers have led many districts to consider privatization of noninstructional functions. A 2006 survey of Michigan's conventional public school districts[ii] by the Mackinac Center for Public Policy found that 37.7 percent of the districts had contracted bus, custodial or food services.[18]

The most common form of school privatization is "contracting," which occurs when a school district signs a contract with a for-profit or nonprofit firm to provide services the district once produced.[iii] Typically,

---

[i] It should be added, however, that state of Michigan payments from the state's school aid fund, which is the primary source for state financing of Michigan elementary and secondary schools, have generally increased, rising by about $1 billion above inflationary growth between 1994-1995 and 2005-2006: see Gary S. Olson and Katherine Summers-Coty, "Analysis of K-16 Funding Initiative," (Michigan Senate Fiscal Agency, 2006), 19, http://www.senate.michigan.gov/sfa/main/sacpresentation0301.pdf, (accessed June 6, 2007).

[ii] I use the phrase "conventional public school districts" to distinguish school districts with publicly elected school boards and conventional school district boundaries from charter schools, which have no publicly elected board and no local tax base, but are also considered school districts under Michigan law.

[iii] Privatization could also include a school district's choosing to no longer provide

such a contract will precisely outline the contractor's responsibilities, the length of the contract and the method of compensation.[iv] Before signing a contract, districts will typically seek competitive bids from firms or organizations that wish to provide the services, a process known as "competitive contracting."

certain services, such as bus or food services. In such instances, parents would become responsible for providing student's food and transportation.

[iv] The contracting process will be discussed in greater detail in "Requests for Proposals, Contracts and Monitoring," Page 41.

The Incidence of Contracting for School Support Services

While there is no official central source of information on the extent to which the nation's more than 14,000 conventional public school districts have privatized support services, there have been several attempts to measure the degree of competitive contracting at various levels of government.[v] What follows is culled from a variety of government, industry and private studies of school service privatization. Despite the inherent survey limitations, the information provides some idea of the extent to which contracting for busing, food and janitorial services occurs in the public school system.

Food Service Contracting

Nationwide, the most detailed set of school privatization statistics involves food service, primarily because the provision of food in schools is highly regulated by the federal government. As a consequence of this federal involvement, state governments track a number of school food service statistics.

In early 2007, a Mackinac Center colleague and I conducted a telephone survey of the 50 state education departments, which keep records concerning all school districts, private schools, religious dioceses and other "school food authorities"[vi] that participate in the federal government's National School Lunch Program.[vii] These data include whether these school food authorities contract with a food service

---

[v] "Table 85, Number of Regular Public School Districts, by Enrollment Size of District: Selected Years, 1990-91 through 2003-04" (National Center for Education Statistics, U.S. Department of Education, 2005). There are also about 4,000 charter, magnet and private schools in the United States.

[vi] A "school food authority" is defined by the National School Lunch Program as "the governing body which is responsible for the administration of one or more schools; and has the legal authority to operate the Program therein *or* be otherwise approved by Food Nutrition Service to operate the Program. See "Child Nutrition Programs, Part 210, National School Lunch Program, Sub-Chapter A," http://a257.g.akamaitech. net/7/257/2422/14mar20010800/edocket.access.gpo.gov/cfr_2003/pdf/7CFR210.2.pdf (accessed April 19, 2007).

[vii] The NSLP was created in 1946 as part of the National School Lunch Act. The program is designed to assist children from low-income families (as well as other individuals) obtain low-cost or no-cost meals in public and private schools, as well as various "residential care" institutions for young people.

management company[viii] for food services provision or management.[ix] Although not every conventional public school district participates in the NSLP, most do, and these NSLP figures thus provide a rough estimate of food service contracting in all conventional public school districts. Our survey asked state officials to tally figures only for conventional public school districts, thereby excluding private, parochial, charter and magnet schools that participate in the NSLP. After the initial survey was complete, we contacted each state a second time to ensure that the initial reports were accurate.

The survey was completed in April 2007 and found that nationwide, approximately 13.2 percent of conventional public school districts participating in the NSLP contract for food services. In Michigan, we found that 28.8 percent of conventional public school districts participating in the National School Lunch Program contracted with a FSMC. This figure ranked Michigan's food service contracting rate fourth highest in the nation, behind Rhode Island (86.1 percent), New Jersey (64.4 percent) and Pennsylvania (36.7 percent).[x]

Six states — Delaware, Hawaii, Kentucky, North Dakota and West Virginia — reported no FSMC contracts. The survey also revealed that

---

[viii] Food service management companies are frequently referred to by the acronym "FSMCs." I use this acronym throughout the primer.

[ix] Researchers have often gathered data concerning NSLP districts through state education departments. For instance, the U.S. General Accounting Office (now the U.S. Government Accountability Office) used this procedure to determine how many NSLP-participating public and private school food authorities were employing FSMCs in fiscal 1995. See "School Lunch Program: Role and Impacts of Private Food Service Companies," (U.S. General Accounting Office, 1996), http://www.gao.gov/archive/1996/rc96217.pdf, (accessed April 17, 2007). Similarly, Price Waterhouse LLP (now Price Waterhouse Coopers LLP), working under a contract with the U.S. Department of Agriculture, contacted state departments of education to determine the number of NSLP-participating public and private school food authorities that were contracting with FSMCs in fiscal 1991. See "Study of Food Service Management Companies in School Nutrition Programs," ed. Food Nutrition Service U.S. Department of Agriculture, Office of Analysis and Education (U.S. Department of Agriculture, 1994).

[x] As measured by student population, the largest food management contracts are located in Illinois, Texas and Georgia. The Chicago Public Schools has more than 400,000 students, and Chartwells School Dining manages the district's citywide food service program. Likewise, Houston and Atlanta school districts contract with private vendors for food service management. The two districts combined have about 259,000 students.

Louisiana and Alabama state laws discourage food service privatization by withholding money.[xi] Nevertheless, there is an exception to the prohibition in Louisiana: the Orleans school district, which is "in the custody of the state" because of the district's poorly performing schools and the problems caused by Hurricane Katrina in 2005.[19] Thus, section 1990 of Part VII of the Louisiana Education of Children with Exceptionalities Act specifically states, "[The] district may contract with for-profit providers for any needed services for a school operated under its jurisdiction."[20]

The state-by-state results are displayed in Graphic 1.

[xi] See La. Rev. Stat. Ann. § 17:194(B), which states, "[N]o state funds shall be disbursed for the support of any school lunch program which shall be used by any private person, enterprise, concern or other entity for profit, regardless of any authority in federal or state law for contracting with such a private supplier or provider of school lunch programs." Legislative language discouraging privatization of school support services has also been passed in Alabama, reducing the amount of contracting there in recent years (Craig Pouncey, assistant state superintendent for financial and administrative services, phone conversation with Michael LaFaive, June 15, 2007).

Graphic 1: Food Service Management Company Use by Conventional Public School Districts in National School Lunch Program, 2006-2007

State	NSLP Districts Contracting Food Services	Total NSLP Districts	Percentage of NSLP Districts Contracting Food Services
Alabama	1	131	0.8%
Alaska	5	50	10.0%
Arizona	44	198	22.2%
Arkansas	0	245	0.0%
California*	2	894	0.2%
Colorado	11	178	6.2%
Connecticut	40	169	23.7%
Delaware	0	19	0.0%
Florida	6	67	9.0%
Georgia	1	180	0.6%
Hawaii	0	1	0.0%
Idaho	4	109	3.7%
Illinois	160	873	18.3%
Indiana	14	294	4.8%
Iowa	8	345	2.3%
Kansas	4	295	1.4%
Kentucky	0	175	0.0%
Louisiana	1	69	1.4%
Maine	2	231	0.9%
Maryland	1	24	4.2%
Massachusetts	47	299	15.7%
Michigan	159	552	28.8%
Minnesota	42	339	12.4%
Mississippi	1	202	0.5%
Missouri	97	524	18.5%
Montana	6	325	1.8%
Nebraska	17	254	6.7%
Nevada	1	17	5.9%
New Hampshire	25	467	5.4%
New Jersey	349	542	64.4%
New Mexico	12	89	13.5%
New York	149	680	21.9%
North Carolina	4	115	3.5%

State	NSLP Districts Contracting Food Services	Total NSLP Districts	Percentage of NSLP Districts Contracting Food Services
North Dakota	0	188	0.0%
Ohio	50	613	8.2%
Oklahoma	15	541	2.8%
Oregon	32	196	16.3%
Pennsylvania	184	501	36.7%
Rhode Island	31	36	86.1%
South Dakota	16	168	9.5%
South Carolina	11	85	12.9%
Tennessee	1	136	0.7%
Texas	96	1,054	9.1%
Utah	2	40	5.0%
Vermont	42	280	15.0%
Virginia	7	132	5.3%
West Virginia	0	55	0.0%
Washington	51	282	18.1%
Wisconsin	61	416	14.7%
Wyoming	3	48	6.3%
Total	**1,815**	**13,723**	**13.2%**

Source: State education departments, author's calculations
* The California data reflect the number of districts that had official contracts with an FSMC to provide services in conventional public school districts. This figure, however, probably understates the role of FSMCs in California. Districts frequently turn to FSMCs through consulting agreements, rather than official contracts. Such agreements were excluded by the state of California when it responded to the survey, while essentially similar agreements were included by other states participating in the survey.

The results dovetail with the findings from surveys of individual states. For instance, researcher Kenneth P. May, working on a 1997 survey of New Jersey superintendents for his doctoral dissertation, found that 65.3 percent of the superintendents responding reported contracting with an FSMC,[21] a figure similar to the 64.4 percent listed for New Jersey's NSLP-participating school districts above.[xii] Recent

---

[xii] Our survey figure is not as close to that of a 2002 New Jersey School Board Association survey, which found that about 54.1 percent of responding New Jersey superintendents reported contracting with an FSMC. See New Jersey School Boards Association, "Subcontracting in the Public Schools Update 2002," (New Jersey: 2002). The NJSBA survey, however, had only a 22.9 percent response rate, compared, for instance, to a 50.9 percent response rate in the May survey described above. Thus, the NJSBA survey, which included districts that do not necessarily participate in the NSLP, involved just

Reason Foundation surveys of conventional public school districts in Florida and Arizona found FSMC contracting rates in 2007 of 10.0 percent and 25.0 percent, respectively,[22] figures similar to the 9.0 percent and 22.2 percent we list for NSLP-participating districts. In addition, a 2002 survey by the Alabama Policy Institute, a Birmingham-based think tank, found that 1.6 percent of the state's conventional public school districts contracted with an FSMC,[23] compared to the 0.8 percent of NSLP-participating districts we list — a difference of just one district. And finally, the Mackinac Center's direct survey of all conventional Michigan public school districts in 2006 concluded that 28.8 percent contracted with FSMCs,[24] a rate equal to the 28.8 percent we determined above using state Department of Education figures for NSLP-participating districts in 2007.[xiii]

Our survey's national figure of 13.2 percent also appears to be in line with other recent national estimates. The U.S. Department of Agriculture, which provides regulatory oversight of the National School Lunch Program, surveyed 2,100 NSLP-participating public school food authorities in the 2003-2004 school year and reached the conclusion that approximately 13 percent were contracting for food services (see Graphic 2).[xiv] In a somewhat different measurement, the national Centers for Disease Control and Prevention in 2000 conducted interviews with food service managers at numerous public, private and parochial schools nationwide and concluded that 16.6 percent were contracting with

----

135 respondents, compared to the 542 districts included in the figures in our survey above. In any case, it is clear that New Jersey districts contract with FSMCs far more frequently than those in almost any other state; even a 54.1 percent FSMC contracting rate would rank the state second in the nation.

[xiii] The 2006 Mackinac Center survey results referred to in this primer differ slightly from the results originally announced in September 2006. Following the initial announcement, additional data were received for three districts, providing figures for all 552 Michigan school districts and leading to small changes in the results. These revised data are the source for the findings reported here.

[xiv] This finding was not published as part of a formal USDA school nutrition study, but was rather part of a public presentation given by USDA in 2006. See Alberta Frost and Patricia McKinney, "FNS School Meals ... Do They Measure Up?," in *School Nutrition Association Annual National Conference* (Los Angeles: United States Department of Agriculture Food and Nutrition Service, 2006).

FSMCs.[xv][25] In response to my request in 2007, the co-author of the CDC study isolated public schools in the study's 2000 dataset and calculated that 15.2 percent of the schools were contracting for food services[26] — a number that makes our calculation of a 13.2 percent contracting rate for conventional public school districts seem plausible.[xvi]

Graphic 2: percentage of NSLP-Participating Public School Food Authorities Contracting with FSMCs Nationwide and by Region, 2003-2004

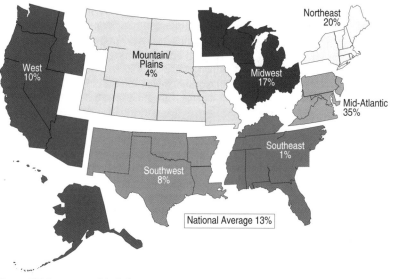

Source: U.S. Department of Agriculture

[xv] Note that this survey dealt with schools, as opposed to school districts or school food authorities.

[xvi] In contrast, a 2005 School Nutrition Association survey of association members in decision-making capacities in public school districts, public schools and private schools found that only 4.5 percent of the responding members said that their school or district contracted with an FSMC for cafeteria services. ("Operations Survey: Final Report," ed. School Nutrition Association (School Nutrition Association, 2005).) This is by far the lowest percentage of food service privatization I have found in any nationwide research, but this may be due to skewing in the composition of the SNA's membership. According to Erik Peterson, director of public awareness for the SNA's Child Nutrition and Policy Center, the low rate at which SNA members report competitive contracting is likely a function of membership characteristics. Peterson notes that SNA members "tend to be self-operated districts and do not contract with management companies." (Erik Peterson, e-mail correspondence with Michael LaFaive, May 2, 2007.)

Privatization surveys also typically show that the primary reason for contracting with FSMCs is cost savings. The Kenneth May study of New Jersey superintendents found that 83 percent of respondents reported that saving money was a "very important" consideration, while 73 percent said that improving operations was.[27] Similarly, a 1995 study by the U.S. General Accounting Office (now the Government Accountability Office) found that around 75 percent of public school food authorities that contracted with FSMCs and that responded to a written questionnaire said reducing costs in their food programs was a "moderate" to "major" reason for contracting.[28]

Surveys also indicate generally positive results from the contracted services. A New Jersey School Board Association survey found that 88 percent of responding superintendents whose districts contracted with FSMCs reported that the resulting food service was either "excellent" or "good," although a relatively low response rate may have skewed this number somewhat.[29] The GAO survey cited earlier reported that districts that contracted with FSMCs experienced an increase in the number of lunches sold.[30]

Capacity of School Food Service Contractors

There are probably two key, interrelated reasons districts decide to contract food services. The first is economies of scale. The ability of large firms like Chartwells School Dining, Aramark School Support Services or Sodexho School Services to make mass purchases of foodstuffs and equipment dwarfs even that of the largest of districts. The resulting price advantages can be difficult to match. Chartwells, for instance, is a subsidiary of the Compass Group, a United Kingdom-based food services company that employs 400,000 people worldwide and provides food services to hospitals, universities, schools and entertainment venues, according to the company's official Web site.[31] Aramark, on the other hand, was large enough to assume the management of food services in the Houston Independent School District, which employed approximately 2,200 food service employees at the time.[xvii]

A second reason for the privatization of school food services may be the government's particularly extensive regulation of school food service

---

[xvii] The Houston contract is discussed in more detail under "Privatization and the Core Mission of Education," Page 27.

programs. The National School Lunch Program, the School Breakfast Program, and the Special Milk Program for Children are highly complex, and a district may wish to contract with a food service management company not just to save money or improve services, but also to delegate to the contractor some of the regulatory compliance burdens.

These regulations can include everything from the proper definition of yogurt ("a coagulated milk product(s)") to the menu choices that high school students must make.[xviii] While federal regulations also place additional mandates on private food service management companies, extensive federal regulation of even in-house school district food services may actually drive districts to contract with vendors that specialize in food services and in compliance with government health and food safety regulations.

Transportation Contracting

Nationwide, school bus transportation involves large expenditures that are distributed among a huge number of providers, both public and private, large and small. The fragmentation is probably due in part to the long-term, grass-roots evolution of the activity. In "Accent on Safety: A History of the National Conference on School Transportation 1939-1985," Ernest Farmer reports that in 1840, children in Massachusetts were the first to be formally transported to schools using public resources.[32] The transportation entailed contracts with farmers[33] to take children to and from school.[xix] The first reference to a school-operated busing program occurs in 1900 in the state of Florida.[34]

[xviii] The NSLP's rules governing high school student food choices are set out below:

> "ii. Offer versus serve. Schools must offer at least three menu items for lunches. Senior high (as defined by the State education agency) school students must select at least two menu items and are allowed to decline a maximum of two menu items. The student must always take the entrée. The price of a reimbursable lunch does not change if the student does not take a menu item or requests smaller portions. At the discretion of the school food authority students below the senior high level may also participate in offer versus serve."

See "Child Nutrition Programs, Part 210, National School Lunch Program, Sub-Chapter A."

[xix] For a fascinating history of pupil transportation, see M.C.S. Noble Jr., *Pupil Transportation in the United States* (Scranton: International Textbook Company, 1940). The book includes a chapter on competitive contracting by public school districts for bus services.

The fragmentation of the private-sector school transportation market is partly responsible for the dearth of national data on the extent of school district contracting with private transportation firms. What researchers are left with is a collection of state-specific research. For instance, according to the nonprofit Connecticut School Transportation Association, 91 percent of transportation for public and parochial schools — 139 of 153 districts in the state — is provided by private vendors.[35] Consultant Robin Leeds states that the same percentage of school transportation is provided by private carriers in Massachusetts.[36] The Massachusetts figure includes private and parochial schools, according to Leeds, but public school districts make up the majority of the contract business.[37]

Estimates of the extent of school transportation contracting are also available from a number of surveys, including many of those cited above under "Food Service Contracting":

- In a 2001 survey of a nationally representative sample of conventional school districts, American School & University magazine found that 31.8 percent of responding districts reported contracting busing services.[38]

- Kenneth May's survey of New Jersey school privatization in 1997 found that 62.2 percent contracted for student transportation.[39]

- The 2002 Alabama Policy Institute study found that 8.1 percent of the Alabama districts that responded to its survey contracted for transportation services to some degree. One of the districts contracted with the county government, which strictly speaking would not qualify as privatization, since the service was not provided by the private sector.[40]

- The Mackinac Center for Public Policy conducted four statewide school privatization surveys in Michigan between 2001 and 2006. The 2006 survey of the state's conventional school districts found that 23, or 4.2 percent, reported contracting with private firms for bus services.[xx][41] This represented a slight increase from 21 districts in 2005.

[xx] This figure does not include contracting for transportation of special education students.

• In the Reason Foundation's 2007 surveys of conventional public school districts in Arizona and Florida, 6.6 percent of Arizona districts reported contracting for student transportation services, while 5.0 percent reported doing so in Florida.

Naturally, each of these surveys involves a risk of "response bias" — that is, the possibility that the districts that choose to respond to the survey are either more likely or less likely than the nonresponding districts to contract with private firms. Nevertheless, the same surveys' results for food contracting agreed well with our food service findings, which had far less risk of response bias, and some of the surveys reached the vast majority of districts,[xxi] reducing the potential impact of response bias.

In any event, the results of these surveys suggest a wide variance in contracting from state to state. Given the American School & University figures, and given the figures cited above for Connecticut, Massachusetts, New Jersey and Alabama, Michigan's 4.2 percent bus service contracting rate for conventional public school districts is probably well below the transportation contracting rate in many other states.

Empirical Studies on Cost Reduction

As noted above, systematic, nationwide data on school bus contracting are scarce, but some state-level analyses exist. Economists E. Bruce Hutchinson and Leila J. Pratt at the University of Tennessee at Chattanooga have twice acquired state data that allowed for a rigorous statistical analysis of school bus contracting costs.

Their first study, published in 1999 in the Policy Studies Journal, involved a comparative analysis of in-house and contracted services for busing in 19 school systems in Tennessee.[42] They found that savings were indeed possible: 15 of the 19 districts had average costs that were 27 percent lower as a result of privatization.[43] At the same time, costs rose by an average of 21 percent in four of the districts following

---

[xxi] For instance, both of the Reason Foundation surveys cited above succeeded in contacting about 90 percent of each of the two states' conventional public school districts. Himebaugh, "Preliminary Brief on Arizona Survey"; Piccolo, "Preliminary Brief on Florida Survey: Contracting School Services." The Mackinac Center's direct survey of conventional school districts in Michigan ultimately gathered data for all 552 districts.

privatization.[44] The research accounted for variables such as the type of buses used, the price of labor and fuel, and what the authors called a "localization factor." The latter was designed to account for such things as differences in the individual contracts, labor rates and geography.[45]

The second study, completed in February 2006 and accepted for future publication in the Journal of Private Enterprise, examined district or "parish" contracting in Louisiana. In this case, Hutchinson and Pratt found that privatized school bus transportation was 10 percent more costly on average than in-house systems. The authors suggest that hybrid systems, where school boards contract for some routes but provide others in-house, may generate savings by retaining less costly bus routes in-house while outsourcing more expensive portions to contractors.[46]

Hutchinson and Pratt's second finding indicates something that will be discussed in more detail later in this primer: Privatization can fail to save money if school districts do not arrange the contracting process to maintain the pressure of monitoring and threat of market competition on the vendor.

Capacity of School Transportation Contractors

Private companies operate approximately 475,000 school buses, according to industry trade journal School Bus Fleet.[47] There are several very large and dominant companies operating in public school districts nationwide, yet there are more than 3,000 individual school transportation firms in all[48] — and even this large number excludes many very small operators.

School Bus Fleet also estimates that as many as 30 percent of all school buses are either owned or operated (or both) by private firms. This figure is derived from data collected each year by the journal from pupil transportation directors in each state government.[49] Steve Hirano, associate publisher of School Bus Fleet, calls this figure a "best guess,"[50] however, and adds that "no one really knows"[51] the complete extent to which public schools contract out for student transportation nationwide.

Robin Leeds, a school transportation expert and consultant with more than 25 years of industry experience, sums up the problem:

> "How large a fleet constitutes a 'company' or a 'contractor?' There are thousands of one-bus owners who contract with school

districts to drive one route; are they included in the count? In Louisiana, for example, 35% of the fleet is privately-owned, but it is primarily these independent owner-operators. One school district, Lafayette Parish, has 150 contractors. So you see the problem. Even if you limit the universe to corporations, for example, or to owners of ten or more buses, there is no central repository of data beyond the 50 or 100 largest companies. It's a guessing game."[52]

According to School Bus Fleet, the 50 largest bus contractors in North America operate more than 107,000 school buses. Forty-five of the 50 largest companies are based in the United States, and the majority of contractors are located on the East Coast, where school transportation contracting appears to be more intense.[53] School Bus Fleet also concludes that Laidlaw Inc. of Naperville, Ill., which transports approximately 2 million students each school day,[54] is the largest school transportation company in North America.[xxii] Laidlaw states that it has 1,000 separate contracts with school districts and parochial schools in the United States and Canada.[55] In contrast, setting aside the one-bus operations described by Robin Leeds above, the small bus companies delivering students to public schools include such operations as Superior Coaches in the city of Hancock, which is located in the Upper Peninsula of Michigan. Superior Coaches operates two school buses, with which it transports 25 students daily.[56]

These figures suggest that a Michigan school district that wishes to solicit bus service bids from private firms will probably find willing bidders even if no local firm seems likely to make an offer.

Custodial Contracting

School contracting for custodial services is even harder to measure than contracting for transportation. I am not aware of a representative nationwide survey of custodial services contracting among public school districts published since the 2001 American School & University survey discussed above.

[xxii] Laidlaw is currently being acquired by FirstGroup, meaning that First Student, a FirstGroup subsidiary, will soon be North America's largest private school bus company.

Therefore, we are left with a single national survey and several state-specific surveys to gauge just how frequently conventional public school districts use contractors in providing custodial work:

- The American School & University magazine's national sample of public school districts in 2001 found that just over 8 percent of respondents contracted with a private firm for custodial work.[57]

- In 2006 in Michigan, the Mackinac Center found that 11.4 percent of the state's conventional public school districts reported contracting for custodial services, an increase of 2.4 percentage points from the previous year.[58]

- A 2000 doctoral dissertation by Barry D. Yost detailed the outcome of his 1999-2000 school year survey of Virginia school districts. In Yost's survey, 9.4 percent of the responding districts reported contracting for custodial services.[xxiii][59] Yost also noted that about 53 percent of respondents said they realized "moderate" to "considerable" savings from contracting.[60]

- In Arizona, the Reason Foundation's 2007 spring survey found that 13.0 percent of conventional school districts contract for custodial services.[61]

- In Florida, the Reason Foundation's 2007 spring survey found that 11 of 60 responding districts (18 percent) contract for custodial services.[62]

Capacity of School Custodial Contractors

While the school transportation industry may have thousands of owner-operators delivering students to school and taking them on field trips, the custodial industry conceivably has tens of thousands of potential vendors because of the low barriers that exist to entering the field.

According to the Building Service Contractors Association International, the industry's trade group, janitorial services of every sort are expected to grow faster than most other service categories. The

---

[xxiii] The survey had a response rate of 64.4 percent. Yost, "Privatization of Educational Services by Contractual Agreement in Virginia Public Schools", 50.

group also points to the federal government's "Service Annual Survey" report which states, "[C]leaning industry receipts increased more than 21 percent from 1999 through 2002." The BSCAI Web site also cites the research and consulting firm Marketdata Enterprises, which predicts that by 2008 the janitorial services industry will be worth more than $128 billion nationwide.[63]

As with the transportation and food industries, the custodial services industry appears capable of meeting any increased demand from school districts for services.

Noninstructional School Service Privatization in Michigan

Graphic 3 shows the results of the Mackinac Center's surveys of Michigan school districts between 2001 and 2006. Although the 2001 survey involved only 250 of Michigan's 552 school districts, the figures suggest an upward trend. The number of conventional school districts contracting bus, food or custodial services reached 37.7 percent in 2006 — roughly three school districts in eight.[xxiv] [64] The approximately 2.2 percentage point increase from 2005 to 2006 represents a 6.2 percent single-year increase in the contracting rate.

Graphic 3: Percentage of Conventional Michigan School Districts Competitively Contracting For Food, Bus or Custodial Services, 2001-2006

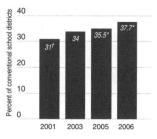

Source: "Survey 2006: School Outsourcing Continues To Grow," Mackinac Center for Public Policy, with author's revisions. Surveys were not conducted in 2002 and 2004.
*†This data was based on a partial sample of districts. *Numbers revised from those originally published.*

[xxiv] The Mackinac Center's 2007 school privatization survey was not complete at the time of publication of this primer.

Graphic 4: Michigan School Districts Contracting Bus, Food or Custodial Services, 2006

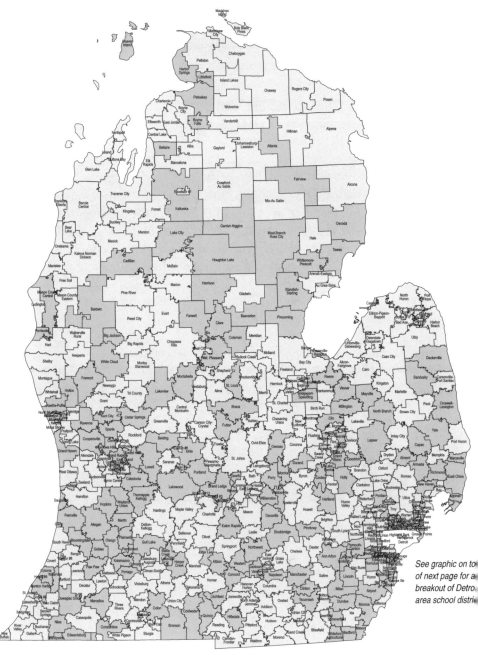

See graphic on top of next page for a breakout of Detroit area school districts

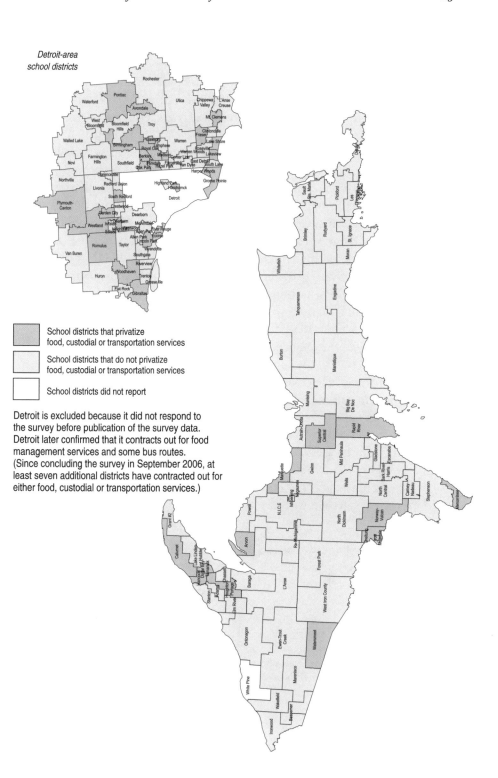

Detroit-area school districts

School districts that privatize food, custodial or transportation services

School districts that do not privatize food, custodial or transportation services

School districts did not report

Detroit is excluded because it did not respond to the survey before publication of the survey data. Detroit later confirmed that it contracts out for food management services and some bus routes. (Since concluding the survey in September 2006, at least seven additional districts have contracted out for either food, custodial or transportation services.)

Food service privatization continues to be a perennial favorite among Michigan districts. According to the 2006 Mackinac Center survey, 159 of Michigan's 552 conventional school districts contracted for food services to some degree — a contracting rate of 28.8 percent.[xxv]

Contracting for custodial services has accelerated in recent years. Mackinac Center privatization surveys in 2005 and 2006 showed year-over-year growth of 26 percent — an increase from 50 districts to 63. Press reports indicated that in 2006, public school districts from Reeths-Puffer in Muskegon to Avondale in Auburn Hills expected to save anywhere from $114 to $128 per student. Jackson Public Schools was reportedly expecting annual savings of $193 per student from their contract with a private provider.[65] In contrast, school transportation in Michigan is still overwhelmingly dominated by public providers.

The Mackinac Center surveys also indicate that the contracting of school support services in Michigan school districts has saved the districts money in the majority of cases. In the 2006 survey, 74.5 percent of Michigan districts that contracted for bus, food or janitorial services said that contracting had yielded savings, while 20.2 percent were unsure and 3.3 percent said it had not. Similarly, 90.9 percent of those districts said they were satisfied with their contracting, and only 5.3 percent said they were not.

Preliminary figures from the 2007 Mackinac Center survey indicate similar results: With 530 of the 552 Michigan districts responding, 79.9 percent have said that contracting saved money, and 90.7 percent said they were satisfied with the results.

[xxv] Chartwells School Dining is clearly the dominant food service contractor in school districts statewide. According to the Mackinac Center's 2006 survey, more than 77 percent of the Michigan districts contracting for food services did so with Chartwells. The survey also showed that the company's closest competitors, Aramark School Support Services and Sodexho School Services, had contracts with 11 districts each, giving each about 7 percent of the districts contracting food service.

Privatization and the
Core Mission of Education

The research recounted above indicates that in many cases, a significant minority — and occasionally a majority — of a state's school districts contract with private firms for the provision of food, bus or custodial services. In Michigan, such privatization has been on the rise.

This finding is not surprising. In every area of life, resources are necessarily limited. Privatization, according to the Mackinac Center school privatization survey, is yielding savings in most districts that contract for bus, food or custodial services. These savings, in turn, free the districts' resources for other goals, including classroom instruction, the districts' core function.

In "Doing More With Less: Competitive Contracting for School Support Services," a 1994 publication of the Mackinac Center and the Reason Foundation, Janet R. Beales neatly sums up why many district officials turn to privatization:

> "In the area of support services, [school] administrators are finding some budgetary relief by turning to the efficiencies of the private sector for help. By contracting with private companies for busing, maintenance, and food service, schools can do more with less. Reducing costs, increasing revenues, and tapping new reserves of capital investment and expertise can help school administrators focus on their core responsibility: educating children."[66]

James Quinn and Frederick Hilmer, writing in the Sloan Management Review in the summer of 1994, argued that an institution needs to focus on what it does best, emphasizing the areas where it has competitive advantages. Doing so, Quinn and Hilmer argued, improves a company's success rate, and they observed that this idea has "been supported by research extending over a twenty year period."[68]

Focusing on "core competency strategies"[67] makes sense even for public school institutions not driven by private-sector profit imperatives. Former U.S. Secretary of Education Rod Paige, while superintendent of the Houston Independent School District, instituted a number of reforms to focus the district on its core function of educating children. In a paper for The Case Program at Harvard University's John F.

Kennedy School of Government, author Kirsten Lundberg described Paige's approach:

> "One of Paige's stratagems for making schools deliver a better educational product was to concentrate on what should be educators' chief expertise — teaching. To do so, he aimed to free the school system from jobs for which it was not especially qualified, such as maintaining buildings, running a bus service and feeding children. Privatization, or outsourcing, such services to private sector contractors would not only save HISD money — in itself a worthwhile goal — but allow HISD administrators and principals to concentrate on educational issues. Paige's leading candidate for privatization was Food Services."[69]

Despite rancorous opposition, Houston managed to privatize. In the summer of 1997, HISD announced that it was awarding Aramark Corp., a professional services company, the contract to manage the district's food service program using the district's approximately 2,200 existing food service employees.[70] In the 1997-1998 school year, the privatization was a considerable financial success, but the food services program experienced losses in its second and third years. "Many of these losses," writes Lundberg, "occurred outside the scope of the contract," including bearing the cost of a district-mandated pay raise for food services staff and the cost of implementing "HISD's new, and expensive, computerized business infrastructure system."[71] In the fourth year, following the implementation of a number of new business practices in coordination with the district, the HISD's privatized food services management was once again saving money. As of 2007, Aramark continued to hold the contract with the HISD.

As the Houston experience suggests, privatization can indeed benefit a district, but monitoring the district's and the contractor's own performance continues to require care. Regardless, districts typically find that managing a contract is less distracting to their educational mission than supervising the production of in-house services. As one Michigan district official said in an early response to the Mackinac Center's 2007 privatization survey, "The more we can get rid of noninstructionally focused services, the more we can focus on instructional services."

Factors Influencing Privatization in Michigan

No matter how much contracting can free a district to focus on its core educational mission, the potential cost savings are usually important, too. As noted earlier under "Contracting of School Support Services" (Page 5), Michigan's school finance structure, which attaches a majority of most districts' money to student enrollment, places an increased premium on schools' cost management.

Proposal A, School Choice and Student Enrollment Trends

This financial dynamic began in 1994, when Michigan voters approved the proposed constitutional amendment known as Proposal A, which created the state per-student "foundation allowance" that ties most districts' operating income closely to student enrollment.[xxvi] From that point on, if a Michigan school district did not continue to attract students, it generally faced stagnant and even declining operating income.[xxvii]

This cost discipline increased in 1995 with the advent of charter schools,[xxviii] which are public schools that are authorized to enroll, and to receive state money for, students living anywhere in the state. (As with conventional public school districts, state money for charter schools takes the form of a per-pupil foundation allowance.[xxix]) Conventional

---

[xxvi] Proposal A also reduced financial disparities among the state's school districts, raised the state sales tax from 4 percent to 6 percent, created a 6 mill state property tax, and lowered property tax rates on most Michigan homes and many other real and personal properties. For further discussion of Proposal A's financial provisions, see Ryan S. Olson and Michael D. LaFaive, "A Michigan School Money Primer for Policymakers, School Officials, Media and Residents," (Mackinac Center for Public Policy, 2007), 5, 24, 39-40, 55, http://www.mackinac.org/archives/2007/s2007-04.pdf, (accessed June 5, 2007).

[xxvii] Income for capital purposes remains independent of state per-pupil monies, since capital spending is financed locally by school district property taxes. Money raised through these taxes for capital purposes cannot be redirected to school operating expenditures, however.

[xxviii] Michigan's original charter school law was passed in 1993, but it faced a substantial court challenge before prospective charter schools began receiving state money under the law. The law was subsequently upheld by the Michigan Supreme Court in 1997, but a second charter school law had already been passed in 1995, and charter schools began to exert competitive pressure on conventional public school districts from then on.

[xxix] Charter schools are authorized to receive state money for their pupils through a revocable "charter" granted by a state university, community college or conventional public school district.

public school districts that lost students to charter schools generally faced a decline in operating revenues.

The cost discipline increased further in 1996, when section 105 of the State School Aid Act was passed to allow conventional school districts to accept a student residing within their intermediate school district and receive state money for the student without the permission of the student's district of residence.[72] This cross-district competition for students, commonly referred to as "school choice" or "schools of choice," expanded again in 1999 with the passage of the State School Aid Act's section 105c, which allowed a conventional public school district to unilaterally accept and receive state monies for students residing in a bordering intermediate school district.[73]

This competition for students and the state monies assigned to them has clear cost implications. For instance, every full-time student who departed a school district in fiscal 2007 represented a financial loss to the district of the district's foundation allowance of $7,085 or more.[xxx] Poorly performing schools districts can thus lose students to other districts or to charter schools, and when large numbers of students leave a district, the financial losses can rise quickly. For example, in a 12-month period ending in the autumn of 2006, Detroit Public Schools lost nearly 14,000 students.[74] This represented an estimated decline of approximately $100 million in operating revenue from foundation allowances alone.[xxxi] Some of that money followed children to other school districts, but not all of it necessarily accrued to conventional public schools and charter schools elsewhere in Michigan. Parents of

---

[xxx]   The foundation allowance associated with a particular pupil varies from district to district. The smallest per-pupil foundation allowance for a district in fiscal 2007 was $7,085, while the allowance exceeded $10,000 in a few districts. The amount of per-pupil state and local operating money that a district receives for a particular student may be less than the foundation allowance, which is not so much an exact amount of money as it is an accounting device. For a detailed discussion of the general foundation allowance and the per-pupil monies actually associated with it, see Olson and LaFaive, "A Michigan School Money Primer for Policymakers, School Officials, Media and Residents," 55-68.

[xxxi]   The Detroit Public Schools' per-pupil foundation allowance in fiscal 2007 is $7,469. Multiply that figure by 13,800 students, and the financial loss to Detroit amounts to $103,072,200. Some federal revenue based on enrollment of "at-risk" students or special education students may also have been lost to the district.

some of these students probably enrolled their children in private or parochial schools, while other parents may simply have moved to other states.

Indeed, parents' incentives to leave the state are likely to increase. Michigan is unique in the economic decline it has experienced since 2001, and residents have been leaving at an increasing rate. According to statistics provided by the United Van Lines moving company, Michigan had the nation's highest rate — tied with North Dakota — of United Van Lines' outbound moves in 2006.[75] A staggering 66 percent of UVL's Michigan client traffic left the state, meaning that just 34 percent of the company's Michigan-related moves were inbound.[76] Last year, Michael J. Hicks, an assistant professor of economics at the Air Force Institute of Technology and an adjunct scholar with the Mackinac Center for Public Policy, performed a statistical analysis of United Van Lines' survey data and found it to be very highly correlated with actual U.S. Census migration data.[77] This makes the UVL numbers something of a leading migration indicator.

Similarly, University of Michigan economists have predicted that the state can expect to lose jobs through 2007 and 2008.[78] This outcome would produce eight straight years of job losses, a streak not seen since the Great Depression.[79]

Declining economic opportunities are likely to lead to lower-than-expected pupil counts. Declining birth rates may do the same. Over the next year, state budget officials project a loss of 15,575 public school students statewide, a decline of 0.93 percent.[80] A Michigan Senate Fiscal Agency memorandum sums up the situation:

> "It is believed the primary reason for this estimated drop in pupil memberships is declining birth rates; in other words, larger classes are exiting the K-12 system than are coming into kindergarten. These declines in pupil memberships, while costing the State fewer dollars, mean, at a minimum, $7,085 fewer for each pupil lost at the local school level."[81]

Personnel Costs

School districts have also faced budget challenges from the cost of school employee pensions, which include a post-retirement health benefit. These pensions, along with those of the employees of charter schools, state colleges and state universities, are financed through the Michigan Public School Employees Retirement System, a state program.

School districts are required to make annual payments into MPSERS to cover the cost of their retired employees pension and health care benefits. In fiscal 2000, this payment was 11.66 percent of a district's total payroll. That percentage, however, climbed to 17.74 percent of payroll in fiscal 2007.[82] The nonpartisan Michigan Senate Fiscal Agency estimated that districts will need to pay about $1,040 per student into the MPSERS system in fiscal 2007 to cover their pension and health care liabilities.[83] The nonprofit Citizens Research Council of Michigan has projected that school districts' MPSERS payments could reach 32 percent of payroll by 2020.[84]

The increase in retiree pension and health care liabilities has increased school districts' incentives to reduce other costs, particularly in districts where operating revenues have been declining, stagnant or growing slowly.

School Districts' Administrative Powers: Public Act 112 of 1994

Michigan law requires that a local board of education negotiate collective bargaining agreements with the exclusive bargaining agents of the district's employees — that is, the district's employee unions. In particular, Michigan law mandates that the local board bargain over the terms and conditions of employment, such as salary and vacation pay.[85]

Under the law, the boards and unions may also bargain over many other issues, such as the district's employee recruiting standards. Such issues are commonly referred to as "permissive" subjects, which have been defined by the Mackinac Center's Thomas W. Washburne and Michael D. Jahr as "[t]hose subjects of bargaining that are not considered mandatory but are not otherwise prohibited [by law]. ..."[xxxii]

Local school districts may not, however, bargain over issues that the

---

[xxxii] Thomas Washburne and Michael Jahr, "A Collective Bargaining Primer for Michigan School Board Members," (Mackinac Center for Public Policy, 2007), 17, http://www.mackinac.org/archives/2007/s2007-01.pdf. Readers interested in a more detailed discussion of mandatory, permissive and prohibited subjects of collective bargaining in Michigan school districts should see Pages 15-20 of that primer.

Michigan Legislature or the state courts have deemed to be "illegal" or "prohibited."[xxxiii] The most important recent legislation concerning these prohibited topics is Public Act 112 of 1994. This law banned, among other items, bargaining over the issue of privatization of "noninstructional" services.[xxxiv] The relevant section follows:

"(3) Collective bargaining between a public school employer and bargaining representative of its employees shall not include any of the following subjects: ...

(f) The decision of whether or not to contract with a third party for 1 or more noninstructional support services; or the procedures for obtaining the contract; or the identity of the third party; or the impact of the contract on individual employees or the bargaining unit."[86]

In other words, the decision to privatize food, bus or custodial services cannot be protested at the bargaining table by, for instance, the teachers union; the decision is left to the local school board alone.

There are few legal judgments interpreting this provision. One question that frequently arises is whether an existing collective bargaining agreement with a noninstructional services union must be honored before contracting can begin.

The answer is unclear. It can be plausibly argued that both the legislative history of the act and the prior case law demonstrate that the Legislature meant to allow school boards to contract at will with private firms for noninstructional services, even in the middle of a collective bargaining contract with public employees for those services.[xxxv] At the same time, it can also be plausibly argued that even if this broader power was the Legislature's subjective aim at the time, lawmakers produced language in Public Act 112 that firmly indicated the contrary. Under

---

[xxxiii] For a list of prohibited topics, see MCL §§ 423.215(3)(a)-(i).

[xxxiv] The law also established new penalties for public employees and their unions if they engage in a strike (public-sector strikes are illegal under Michigan law).

[xxxv] For instance, State Sen. Mike Prusi of Michigan's Upper Peninsula told The (Marquette) Mining Journal in May 2007, "Right now, a school can basically terminate an agreement with their employees and outsource the work if someone underbids the contract." See Sam Eggleston, "Critics Knock Prusi Bill," *The (Marquette) Mining Journal*, May 7, 2007. Sen. Prusi has introduced legislation that would strike out the provision of the law quoted above.

this view, although the act prohibits collective bargaining over the decision to contract noninstructional services with a private firm, the act does not in any way prohibit public employees from providing those noninstructional services. Hence, a contract with public employees for the provision of noninstructional services is legal (insofar as the contract deals with the basic terms of employment[xxxvi]) and cannot be ignored.

School districts seeking to contract services during the term of a collective bargaining agreement with the relevant noninstructional services union should seek legal counsel. Regardless, it seems clear that as long as existing agreements with noninstructional service employee unions are honored to their conclusion, a school board is free to contract for the provision of a noninstructional service. The contracting process and its impact on union employees need not — and in fact cannot — be collectively bargained.

[xxxvi] If, however, a bargaining agreement contained a provision that did not pertain to the employment relationship — for example, a provision that barred the school district from establishing procedures for competitively contracting noninstructional work — this provision would not be enforceable, since it would involve a prohibited subject of bargaining.

School Privatization
Contracting Guide

Contracting has been a feature of western civilization for millennia; one privatization researcher has noted that the ancient Greeks contracted for removal of resources from publicly owned forests and mines.[87] Nevertheless, experience has shown that contracting can sometimes fail and can also be controversial. The balance of this primer discusses what steps can be taken to facilitate sound bidding and monitoring of a contract for school transportation, food or custodial services.

The first critical element in good contracting is understanding the contracting process itself, beginning with the "Request for Proposal." An RFP is an official document issued by the school district to solicit bids from private vendors for a particular service, in light of the service specifications and contract criteria set forth in the RFP itself. An RFP, then, invites potential vendors to submit bids that offer to meet or exceed the district's quality expectations at a competitive price.[xxxvii]

Requests for Proposals, Contracts and Monitoring

The following is a general description of key components of a Request for Proposal. The discussion below also includes explanations of important contracting words, phrases and concepts.

This summation should help the reader better understand the contracting process and should make RFPs easier to understand for district officials contemplating privatization. A good RFP, in turn, will make the contract easier to write and will help produce a more effective contract monitoring process.

Several points should be made about an RFP before considering its contents. An RFP and the subsequent bidding process usually involve vendors who are for-profit businesses, but not always. Iron Mountain Public Schools in the Upper Peninsula of Michigan contracts for food services from Dickinson Area Catholic Schools, the local Catholic school system.[88] Moreover, one "not-for-profit" bidder is implicitly present in all school district privatizations: the school district employees who currently provide the school support service. As a practical matter, they are usually "competing" with potential private vendors as soon as the

---

xxxvii   Hence, an RFP is not an "Invitation to Bid." An invitation to bid (or "invitation for bid") is generally intended to elicit the lowest possible price for a specific good or service. In contrast, an RFP and the subsequent bidding are meant to promote a high quality of service as well as a low price.

district's intention to privatize is announced, since school employee unions will often offer wage, benefit and work-rule concessions to entice the district to forgo competitive contracting with private firms.[xxxviii]

Another point: An RFP must be informative. A school district uses this document to tell vendors what it wants and when. The instructions are often very detailed, but a well-written RFP does not include language so restrictive that it unnecessarily limits the number of vendors who might bid on a contract.

For example, an RFP that unrealistically limits the time in which a contractor is expected to take over an entire service may exclude most bidders from participating in the process. An experienced vendor has a good sense of how much time is needed to ensure a smooth transition. Demanding a turnover of school transportation responsibilities in just two months when the vendor knows this to be unrealistic will result in failed attempts to secure a capable vendor.

Contents of a Request for Proposal

Any school district that wishes to design its own RFP from scratch should purchase a guide entitled "How to Develop Your Request for Proposal," published by the California-based Brandon Hall Research.[xxxix][89] This paper, the best of its kind, describes the basic contents of an RFP and includes an example of an RFP for a hypothetical bread company interested in acquiring a "Learning Management System." The book's RFP outline is reprinted in Graphic 5 with the permission of Brandon Hall.

[xxxviii]   Another possibility is that the school district's employees will be invited to submit a formal bid in the competitive contracting process. Such an approach does occur in the privatization of other government services, such as regional transit, but it is uncommon among Michigan school districts. One challenge in any such public-private competition is ensuring that the cost of the public employees' provision of the service is fully accounted for, so that the district realizes genuine savings and the public employees are bidding on a level playing field with private contractors. For instance, the cost to heat a school workshop where school bus repairs are performed would need to be included in a public school transportation employees' bid, as would other service-related capital costs that may well be hidden in the district's current accounting scheme.

[xxxix]   "How to Develop Your Request for Proposal" is available for purchase through the company's Web site at www.brandon-hall.com.

Graphic 5: Outline of an RFP (Developed by Brandon Hall Research)

I. Introduction
    A. Overview of the company[xl]
    B. Overview of the opportunity
    C. RFP goals

II. Instructions for responding
    • Bid submission and award notification
    • Number of copies, submission deadline and timeline
    • Confidentiality
    • Questions and answers

III. Basis of award
    (1) Quality of service and track record of results
    (2) Service orientation and project management skills
    (3) Financials (statement of work and pricing)
    (4) Implementation and transition plan
    (5) Innovation and management information services

IV. Proposal duration

V. Additional considerations
    • Liabilities
    • Audits
    • Confidentialities

VI. Scope of services, service levels and related requirements
    • Strategic partnership
    • Measurement and evaluation
    • System and software compatibility
    • Quality and performance guarantees
    • Invoicing
    • Activity reporting
    • Project team
    • Continuous improvement
    • Other

VII. References

VIII. Award duration

IX. Contract terms

Appendices
    A. Assignment of intellectual property and nondisclosure agreement[xli]
    B. Request for information
    C. Standard contract terms and conditions[90]

[xl] In the contracting of school support services, the "company" referred to here would be the school district.

[xli] This section would not apply in the case of school support services, but an appendix might instead deal with the ultimate ownership of certain property used in the provision of the service.

Districts that are interested in using ready-made RFPs that have been employed successfully in Michigan can easily do so. Working jointly, Michigan School Business Officials, the Michigan Association of School Administrators and the Michigan Institute for Education Management have collected and posted at www.schoolpurchasingpages.org a wide variety of contract-related documents, including RFPs for the three main school services discussed in this primer:

- Food services (http://www.schoolpurchasingpages.org/ staticcontent/doclibrary/ProducePurchaseBidProposal.pdf)[xlii]

- Bus services (http://www.schoolpurchasingpages.org/ staticcontent/doclibrary/StudentTransportationServices.pdf)

- Custodial services (http://www.schoolpurchasingpages.org/ staticcontent/doclibrary/CustodialServicesContract-RFP.pdf)

These "School Purchasing Pages" RFPs will be referred to in the discussions of RFPs below. Readers interested in other examples of Michigan school districts' RFPs can inspect a number that have been posted to the Mackinac Center's Web site. The Web addresses for these RFPs appear in "Appendix 2: Sample RFPs, Company Responses and Contracts," Page 87.[xliii]

RFPs for Transportation Services and Custodial Services

Below are descriptions of the key features of a standard RFP. The list of features corresponds to many of those found in the custodial and busing RFPs posted on the School Purchasing Pages Web site. Both of these SPP RFPs have been adapted and used to some degree by Michigan school districts.

Food service RFPs have many of the same provisions found in custodial and busing RFPs, but nonetheless require separate treatment. The federal and state role in food services is so extensive that it is not possible to incorporate a summary of a food service RFP into the

---

[xlii] As will be discussed below, RFPs for food services must conform closely to state and federal guidelines. The sample RFP cited here was in conformity with those guidelines, but may now be outdated. Districts interested in contracting for food services should make sure they have received the most recent recommended RFP from the state.

[xliii] The Web version of this primer has live hyperlinks for all of the items listed in Appendix 2; see www.mackinac.org/8640.

following description without doing a disservice to the subject. RFPs for food services are discussed in "RFPs for Food Services," Page 52.

The Cover Letter

An RFP sent to potential vendors may be prefaced with an explanatory letter that sums up the district's intent. The letter may also include such details as the length of the proposed contract, explicit instructions for responding and the requirement that vendors attend a pre-bid conference meeting to receive additional information and to raise any questions the vendors may have for district officials.

In 2005, Gobles Public Schools issued an RFP to partially privatize its custodial services. The district's cover letter noted that the district's school board had already voted to privatize and was now simply selecting the right vendor.[91] It gave the date of a mandatory pre-bid meeting and the deadline for submitting bids. The signer of the letter also promised to outline for each vendor the district's "current situation" and to arrange a tour of the district's facilities.[92] The cover letter was followed by a 22-page RFP.

Introductory Information

RFPs typically begin with the most important information and become more detailed as they progress. The opening sections emphasize vital information, such as contact data for the project manager and the deadline for a bid submission. The introduction will also tell vendors when proposals will be opened, an important step in which all the original bids are revealed to the public simultaneously to prevent a district official from privately opening the bids and informing a vendor how to alter its bids to ensure it wins. Items in this introduction may also appear in the cover letter and in the timeline discussed below.

One competitive contracting concept not yet addressed often appears in the RFP'S introductory section: "bid bonds," or some other device for ensuring a bidder is genuinely committed during the bidding process. For instance, in the absence of a monetary penalty, a company might be tempted to draw up a proposal in haste with the idea of withdrawing the bid later if it becomes clear the bid was ill-advised. Such behavior would waste the district's time and resources. By submitting a bid bond (usually equivalent to 5 percent of a total bid) in conjunction with the proposal, the company provides the district with some insurance against the company's withdrawing its bid later. Bidders that did withdraw their proposals would then forfeit their bond to the district to compensate the district for lost time, while other bidders would have their bond returned.[xliv][93]

The School Purchasing Pages RFP for busing services mentioned above (see Page 44) contains a few differences from the outline provided here. First, the SPP RFP spells out up front how the proposals submitted by vendors will be "scored" by the district. For instance, the cost of the service will count for 45 percent of the overall evaluation in choosing a new vendor; experience will count for 15 percent; and so on. The authors of this RFP recognize that these criteria will be judged somewhat subjectively and say so in the text, but a degree of subjective judgment is hard to avoid in evaluating RFPs, because price is only one component of overall value. Second, the SPP RFP prohibits contractors with less than five years' experience from participating in the bidding.

Definitions

This section of the RFP is usually straightforward, and district business officers who have done any contractual work will be familiar with it and with most of the terms being defined. Definitions are placed into RFPs (and later into contracts) to ensure that all parties have the same understanding of the meaning of the contract terms. Nine words or phrases that appear in the SPP RFP for custodial services are "district," "contractor," "proposal," "custodial service," "properties," "contract," "accounting period," "contract year," and "district representative."[94]

The SPP RFP for transportation contains no such definitions, nor were these used by Tecumseh Public Schools when it adapted that RFP during a competitive contracting process. Instead, Tecumseh defined these terms later in its 2006 contract for bus services with the First Group of America Corporation. Some general words like "district" and "contractor" appear in the Tecumseh contract, but also appearing are

---

[xliv] A bid bond is not the same as a "performance bond," which is essentially an insurance policy in which the insurer guarantees to find a new service provider if a contractor is unable to continue providing the service for the entire term of the contract. Flam and Keane, *Public Schools Private Enterprise: What You Should Know and Do About Privatization*, 110.

more specialized terms, such as "bus driver," "special trips" (like field trips), and "specifications."[95] These "specifications" encompass important details and may include items described under "District Demands and Specifications" below.

District Demands and Specifications

At some place in the RFP body or in a separate appendix, district officials need to lay out critical information that vendors will use to make price estimates for their bids. This can begin with general descriptions like the contract terms and the location of district buildings, but it will often go into more detailed demands concerning the equipment to be used and other bidding specifications (as it does, for instance, in the SPP RFP for custodial services[xlv]).

Some specifications sections will be less specific. In the Tecumseh Public Schools RFP, the district uses the specifications section to *ask* for information. For instance, the district instructs the vendor to describe how large the vendor's bus fleet will be, what the vendor's "processes for establishing routes and interacting with district personnel" will be and how the vendor intends to handle pupils who misbehave. By contrast, the specifications section in the SPP RFP for custodial services actually lists what requirements the district expects the vendor to adhere to in creating its bid.

Scope of Work

There is arguably no more important section of the RFP — and ultimately the contract — than the "scope of work." In "Doing More With Less: Competitive Contracting for School Support Services," Janet Beales described eight critical expectations that a district should explain in its RFP's scope of work section. They are worth reprinting here:

- "Service Parameters that provide a detailed description of the specific services requested. For example, a contract for custodial services might specify that the contractor provide cleaning

---

[xlv] The term "specification(s)" actually appears twice in the SPP RFP for custodial services — once in Section III ("Specifications/Scope of work") and once in Section VIII ("Contract specifications"). In contrast to the specifications in Section III, the specifications in Section VIII focus on the expected service quality.

equipment and supplies, a certain number of employee-training hours, and supervisory personnel.

- Quality Standards that describe the level of quality which must be met by the provider. For example, a contract for food service would specify requirements such as minimum nutritional requirements for meals, sanitary conditions, and menu variety.

- Backup or substitute requirements if the contractor is unable to provide a service.

- Insurance and Bonding Requirements. Performance bonding is a type of financial insurance for schools should the contractor fail to perform and the school be forced to obtain replacement services.

- Permits and Licenses.

- Reporting and data requirements.

- Personnel Requirements.

- Quality Assurances. This is often expressed as a guarantee to the school district by the contractor that certain expectations will be met. For example, a food-service contract may specify that the contractor will absorb any losses related to the operation of the schools' cafeterias."[96]

It should be added that the scope of work is sometimes more general, with details left to specifications provided later in the document. For instance, the Midland Public Schools recently awarded Grand Rapids Building Services a contract to provide custodial services, and in soliciting potential bidders, the district assembled what may be one of the most detailed sets of work specifications extant in Michigan's public school system today.[xlvi][97] These specifications appear, however, in exhibits appended at the end of the document. Regardless, such precision greatly decreases the possibility that any detail is left to chance or rests on differing assumptions. The resulting clarity can help ensure against future disagreements.

[xlvi]   See "Appendix 2: Sample RFPs, Company Responses and Contracts" for the Web address of the Midland Public Schools RFP.

In the mid-1990s, the Pinckney Community Schools found itself at least temporarily liable for charges its contractor submitted for doing work that was allegedly outside the scope of the contract to which the contractor had agreed. Even if this was just a misunderstanding between the district and the contractor, it amounted to an expensive and sometimes embarrassing misunderstanding.

Procurement Timetable

Some RFP authors choose to include a timetable like the one listed in Graphic 6 (Page 65). These are optional, however, because RFPs usually include important dates, such as pre-bid meetings and vendor presentations, somewhere in the document. The table is simply a helpful summation.

Requirements of Proposal

This section explains what information a vendor must put in its proposal and the manner and format in which the proposal should be submitted. These requirements may span a few pages of the RFP and include (but not be limited to) the following:

- Prepare a proposal that can be easily converted into a contractual agreement;

- Demonstrate that the vendor understands the job necessities, and detail the vendor's experience in the field;

- Spell out the precise length of the contract as stipulated by the RFP;

- Detail a transition plan that includes a description of staff;

- Describe the company's management philosophy and organizational chart;

- Describe training employed for the vendor's management-level staff.[xlvii]

- List vendor-owned equipment to be used throughout the district;

[xlvii] For instance, the SPP RFP for custodial services mandates that the custodial staff be trained in handling biohazards and asbestos. "School Purchasing Pages Custodial RFP," 9.

- Include a description of costs for everything from staff salaries and wages to insurance and banking costs.

- Provide a cover letter that highlights the main features of the proposal;

- List at least one vendor client who has parallel service needs to the district issuing the RFP; and

- Submit a stipulated number of copies of the signed proposal.

In the SPP RFP for custodial services, the vendor is also told to update the equipment list as the equipment changes or face stiff penalties: "This information will be constantly updated and all equipment not listed will be considered District property."[98]

Evaluation Criteria

This section describes the process that will be used to judge which bidder has the most attractive proposal after the submitted bids are opened by the school district. Steps can and should be taken to ensure this process is as objective as possible, and district officials should explain in this section of the RFP what those steps will be.

For instance, as noted earlier, the SPP RFP for transportation services puts 45 percent of the emphasis on price, 15 percent each on "experience," "reliability" and "operational plan," and 10 percent on "expertise of personnel." These factors are weighed only if all the other bidding mandates in the RFP are met.[99]

In contrast, the SPP RFP for custodial services lists vendor experience and the price of the service as two of nine criteria, but does not explain how much each will be valued.[100]

Contract Specifications

The specifications in this section describe service performance mandates to which the winning contractor must adhere. This section is often used to anticipate and thwart any performance problems that may arise once the contract is signed.

The mandates in this section run from the mundane, such as the wearing of staff uniforms and prohibitions on disturbing the personal property of school staff, to more extensive requirements, such as meeting all applicable health and safety laws or conducting thorough background checks and drug screening of contractor staff. The SPP RFP for custodial services even requires a description by the contractor of the company's "corporate commitment to recycling."[101] This RFP also includes details meant to facilitate contract monitoring, such as asserting the district's right to conduct inspections of the custodial work; requiring the contractor to provide financial data; and prohibiting the winning contractor from using the district in the contractor's advertising without the district's express permission.

Terms

The SPP RFP for custodial services concludes with a detailed list of "general terms and conditions"[102] containing warnings that the contractor must comply with government laws and regulations. They include such items as the following:

- obtaining all permits and licenses necessary to perform such duties;

- paying any taxes on the equipment used (and any other taxes) in the discharge of contractor responsibilities;

- adhering to equal employment laws, rules, regulations and government employment mandates;

- satisfying all applicable provisions of the U.S. Occupational Safety and Health Act; and

- complying with requirements of the federal Family Education Rights and Privacy Act.[103]

This section also includes very important specifications about the type and value of insurance that the contractor must maintain throughout the contract period for everything from worker's compensation to auto liability and property damage.[104]

Note that exhibits and addenda can be added to an RFP to spell out any additional contract specifications that are not covered in the main body of the RFP. Exhibit 2 of the SPP RFP for custodial services, for instance, details cleaning frequencies and is followed by the specific physical addresses of each building that must be cleaned.[105] The effect is to leave as little as possible to chance.

RFPs for Food Services

Because of the dominant role that the federal government plays in financing and regulating school food services, there is much less discretion in the way districts create an RFP and the way FSMCs operate the district's service. In fact, the district doesn't create an RFP so much as it just fills in the blanks of the one given to it by state government.

Elsewhere in the nation, it is fairly easy to obtain the official food service RFP or IFB documents on each state's official Web site (usually the department of education's site). In Michigan, the RFP and related documents are not posted on the Web. School districts interested in obtaining the documents must contact the state supervisor for grants coordination and school support at the Michigan Department of Education to acquire the official RFP and instructions for seeking bids on district food services. Once a request is made, the Michigan Department of Education will send an electronic message to the recipient with a 32-page Microsoft Word® document and a 16-sheet Microsoft Excel® spreadsheet.[xlviii]

The state's package of material comes with instructions and a letter of introduction for the recipient. The letter emphasizes a number of points that are worth expanding here.

First, changes to the prototype document provided by the state can be made, but they must be made in bold "and brought to the attention of potential bidders."[106] Second, the federal government mandates that contracts with an FSMC be no longer than one year, but with an option to renew four times for one-year only each — an RFP stipulation deemed important enough by the state to be mentioned in the opening paragraph of the state's official cover letter. Third, emphasis is placed on four key "certification sheets" that must be submitted by the winning bidder:

(1) The Clean Air & Water sheet is a one-page document signed by the FSMC representative that states the FSMC explicitly agrees to comply with pertinent sections of the Clean Air Act and Federal Pollution Control Act; that none of the FSMC

[xlviii] The Mackinac Center has posted these documents on its Web site (see Appendix 2), but they should be reviewed for general purposes only. The documents are dated October 2006, and since the contents are subject to change, district officials preparing to contract with a food services vendor should obtain the latest version of the RFP from the Michigan Department of Education.

operations will occur in buildings on the "EPA List of Violating Facilities"; that the FSMC will work hard to adhere to the clean air and water standards and to include in any subcontracts the material parts of the Clean Air Act and Water Act to which the main contractor is required to adhere.[107]

(2) The Independent Price sheet is designed to certify that the FSMC has not effectively colluded with a fellow competitor over the issue of prices.[xlix][108]

(3) The Lobbying sheet is reasonably self-explanatory. Bidders are prohibited from lobbying the government using federal monies provided for food services (though the contractors are free to lobby using profits they may realize on a contract).[109]

(4) The Debarment and Suspension certification is evidence that the vendor has not been prohibited from being party to this particular deal by the federal government.[110]

The state's cover letter also explicitly notes that when a district is choosing a food services contractor, the price of the services must exceed 50 percent of the weight given to all variables in the district's decision-making process.[111] In other words, the district must choose a contractor based mostly, though not exclusively, on price.

In addition to reading the state's materials on food services contracting, district officials interested in the subject should obtain and read sample food-service RFPs from neighboring districts. Similarly, they should also review FSMC-related questions and answers from the U.S. Department of Agriculture's Food and Nutrition Service (see Appendix 2 for links to these). This USDA agency routinely receives questions from school food authorities nationwide and typically compiles those questions and the FNS responses and posts them on the USDA Web site. Subjects cover everything from buying "American" (a stipulation of the National School Lunch Program) to "guaranteed returns" (money an FSMC promises to return to the district from its food service

---

[xlix] As will be described below under "10 Contracting Rules of Thumb," one Upper Peninsula school district that contracts for bus services nevertheless maintains two district buses to increase the competition between vendors. Such practices can undermine any collusion over prices among vendors.

revenues) to the prohibition of contracts to vendors that write the RFP specifications or other documents themselves.[112] These explanations can help a district avoid pitfalls in the contracting process.

One item in the preceding paragraph should be respected in particular: A district should not let a vendor help write the specifications that will be used in the district's RFP. Given the complexity of food services contracting, seeking help from a vendor may be tempting, but aside from being prohibited by the federal government,[1] this approach can lead to a badly skewed result. After all, vendors may suggest specifications that effectively thwart their competitors, rather than facilitate the beneficial competition the district seeks.

Finally, districts should also resist the temptation to replace an RFP with an "invitation for bid," which is meant solely to solicit the lowest price. Most districts in Michigan already use RFPs, but it is worth stressing here that an RFP gives the district and its officials the opportunity to build a working relationship with a vendor over service quality. While price is important in choosing a vendor (recall that it must amount to at least 50 percent of the decision in food service contracts), price is not the only consideration. Also important are quality improvements and the ability to work with a good vendor over time.

Opposition to Privatization

The previous section dealt with numerous technical aspects of the competitive bidding process. As important as those issues are to successful privatization, however, a discussion of the contracting of school support services would be incomplete without a discussion of opposition to privatization. Employees of a district considering

---

[1] Consider the following from a stern USDA memo on the subject:

"In October 2001, we asked our Regional Offices to advise their respective State agencies that [USDA] regulations prohibit the awarding of contracts to any entity that develops or drafts specifications, requirements, statements of work, invitations for bids, requests for proposals, contract terms and conditions or other procurement documents. ... We continue to receive complaints of SFAs using a prospective bidder to draft specifications and procurement documents and feel that this potential continued noncompliance with Department regulations warrants our addressing the issue directly with the respective State agencies."

See Garnett, "School Districts and Federal Procurement Regulations," 1.

privatization will naturally be concerned about their future employment. Their union, in addition to its concern for the workers, will face the prospect of fewer union jobs and fewer dues-paying members. Indeed, a public fight with the opponents of privatization is almost guaranteed once a district's intent to competitively contract is known.

This fight can be surprisingly harsh — and not just in big districts accustomed to rough-and-tumble politics. In 2000 and 2001, the Arvon Township Public Schools, with an 11-member student body, debated privatizing transportation, food and janitorial services that were costing up to 38 percent of the district's $260,000 budget.[113] Contracting would have cut about 30 percent from the cost of providing the services in-house.[114] Arvon's district officials stated that they had hoped to use the savings for a school improvement program.[115]

Mary Rogala, then president of the Arvon district's board of education, reported that the board began experiencing trouble from the moment it announced its intention to privatize. The Michigan Education Association, a school employees union that represented five Arvon employees, served the Board with an unfair labor practices complaint and took the district to court.[116]

Despite the opposition, the board approved the privatization plan on a 3-2 vote. Shortly after this vote, Rogala recounted, one member called a special meeting to rescind his vote after saying that a number of threats had been made against him and his business.[li][117] This reversal temporarily forced the board to abandon the privatization.

Passions will also run high at board meetings. Shouts, catcalls and angry language are common, and the meetings are made more uncomfortable by the larger turnout and the probable presence of reporters and television cameras.

National Education Association Opposition

There is also a stored fund of anti-privatization rhetoric and tactics that will probably be brought to bear against a district that is publicly investigating competitive contracting. The National Education Association, the nation's largest school employees union, has produced anti-privatization guides and been a vociferous opponent of school

---

[li] A five-minute Mackinac Center video of this story is posted at http://www.mackinac .org/3397.

privatization. One of the association's most recent anti-privatization publications is titled, "Beat Privatization: A Step-by-Step Crisis Action Plan."[118] School board members, superintendents and business officers should have a copy of this publication, since it indicates the kinds of questions and criticisms decision-makers are likely to hear in public debate.

The NEA guide contains a 10-step plan for opposing privatization and a "tool kit" for recording useful board meeting information, such as committee names, committee meeting schedules, people scheduled to make presentations to the board, and (the guide adds), any "gossip, tidbits, whatever, picked up before, during, and/or after the meeting."[119] The final page of this particular guide includes four pieces of artwork for buttons and stickers for "distribution to education support professionals threatened by privatization and their supporters." One of these reads, "I work here! I live here! I vote here! I am the TAXPAYER."[120]

The guide also includes arguments that the NEA suggests privatization opponents use against supporters. These items are "talking points" that can be quickly deployed in public debate. For instance, in the NEA manual's "Tool H" section, entitled "The Pro and Con Debate: Countering Arguments that Support Subcontracting,"[121] strong rhetoric is deployed, with references to "inexperienced, transient workers with few benefits and receiving minimum wages," "faceless, nameless employees," and "[s]trangers in our schools [who] are hazardous to everyone's health and well-being."

School district officials should recognize that some of the arguments they hear may be part of a calculated campaign abetted by a highly organized labor union. Other national anti-privatization sources that officials may wish to familiarize themselves with include the following:

- The American Federation of Labor and Congress of Industrial Organizations' 1993 publication, "The Human Costs of Contracting Out: A Survival Guide for Public Employees."[lii]

[lii] Krista Schneider, "The Human Cost of Contracting Out: A Survival Guide for Public Employees" (Public Employee Department, AFL-CIO, 1993). For a description of this product and responses to its salient features, see Michael LaFaive, "Labor Pains," (Mackinac Center for Public Policy, 1997).

- The American Federation of State, County and Municipal Employees' monograph "Schools for Sale: The Privatization of Non-Instructional School Services."[122]
- The National Education Association Online Resources' "Privatization Problems Make News."

Michigan Education Association Opposition

The Michigan Education Association, which is the primary school employees union in most Michigan public schools districts, is a state affiliate of NEA. The MEA can thus act as a conduit for the national union's efforts. For instance, the "10-step plan" for fighting privatization published in the Spring 2007 edition of the union's newsletter, MEA Voice, contains material that is adapted from the NEA "Beat Privatization" guide described above.[123]

The MEA also mounts powerful opposition independent of the national union. The MEA has long opposed contracting in the school districts with which it bargains. Like the NEA, it has produced anti-privatization work. This material is not particularly easy to obtain, but an idea of the contents of one such publication, the 1995 pamphlet "Privatizing Public School Services: The Rest of the Story," can be gleaned from my essay "Setting the Privatization Record Straight," available at http://www.mackinac.org/2141.[124]

The MEA has also made a science of tough negotiation. Consider comments made in an MEA union negotiator training tape:[125]

- "Do your best to split the board on crucial issues through contacts with individual board members or misrepresentation of the issues to the public through press releases. Attempt to carefully attack the credibility of the board negotiating team so that most of the board team's executive sessions with their board will be spent answering board members' questions about association charges and not with planning on upcoming negotiation sessions."[126]

- "Remember that large districts rely heavily upon the superintendent to absorb the flak. They use the superintendent as a shield. If he is discredited, the rest of the board suddenly feels naked, and they are often eager to take an escape route which the association has waited for the appropriate moment to offer."[127]

- "Use time as an ally. You know, if your negotiating team can get to bargaining sessions well rested, whereas the board's team is harried and fatigued, keep negotiations going until 2 o'clock or 3 o'clock in the morning. Wear down the board physically and psychologically."[128]

The tape also suggests that negotiators investigate the background of each school board member, including religious affiliation, marital status, age, education, employment, family, politics, "his relationship with his employer or employees" and whether "holding a public office help[s] him advance in his job or produce business connections. ..." According to the tape, such information means the negotiator will "know what sensitive chords and nerves to hit during negotiation to get the results you seek."[129]

Responses to Anti-Privatization Claims

In the face of such tactics, school district officials will not just want to follow sound contracting and planning procedures, but be prepared to respond to commonly expressed concerns about privatization. There are straightforward and effective responses to the broad arguments usually posed against privatizing school support services. Consider the anti-privatization arguments below and the responses that follow.

The Claim That Private Firms Will Hire Unqualified Workers

First, a contractor has every incentive to hire the districts' current employees because of their expertise and institutional knowledge. Such workers are unlikely to be "transient." Moreover, districts often ask vendors to give preference to current employees when hiring new staff to provide services under the contract. That's precisely what happened in Midland in 2007, and it is common in other districts as well.

Second, the bidding process can also include a consideration of the experience and qualifications of a private vendor's staff. Firms proposing to use unqualified personnel can be dismissed from consideration long before a contract is awarded. A district with a well-written contract can also exercise a cancellation clause to penalize a contractor that violates a district's personnel qualification requirements.

The Claim That Private Firms Will Hire Low-Wage Workers

The accusation that contractors pay low wages should be challenged with a comparative analysis. Vendors frequently offer to pay new employees wages that are identical to comparable public school employees' wages.

The difference comes in the value of the employee benefits, such as pensions and health care benefits. Indeed, this area of public school personnel costs is so expensive and growing so rapidly that it may actually be the primary motive in districts' decision to privatize. Bargaining units could probably pre-empt more competitive contracting initiatives by offering to give up their expensive benefit packages in favor of the more modest alternatives received by most private-sector workers.[liii]

The Claim That Private Firms Will Hire Dangerous Workers

The alleged risk to children from hiring a private vendor does not withstand scrutiny. Private vendors have no economic incentive to see children come to harm as a result of their or their employees' actions. Quite the opposite is true; indeed, it's difficult to imagine anything more damaging to a contractor's business with its various public school clients than having a dangerous employee put a child at risk. Millions of dollars of business, potential lawsuits and even the company's survival would be at stake.

Moreover, districts commonly emblazon security measures into RFPs and contracts. Some may demand that vendors conduct security measures at a level identical to or exceeding the district's own requirements for its employees; the School Purchasing Pages RFP for transportation services, for instance, requires criminal background checks and alcohol and drug testing.[130] Other districts may demand the right to conduct the security checks themselves with information provided by the vendor on each employee. In addition, districts can

---

[liii] Public school employee benefits will likely be the next big area of competitive contracting or of state-mandated reform. Many districts simply will not be able to sustain the cost of paying school employee health care plans that are not just unusually generous, but even more unusually expensive.

demand the right to have an employee removed from a site after the contract is in place.[liv]

Moreover, there is nothing inherent in public service or private employment that makes one person a better human being than another. There is no reason for private-sector workers to be impugned simply because they work for a private company.

Unions will seek out anecdotal evidence of wrongdoing by the employees of private vendors and try to build a case against privatization based on these examples. But similar examples abound for public school employees, and it is not hard to find them.[lv] District officials may be compelled to recite a few of these examples to remind residents that neither public- nor private-sector employees are unfailingly virtuous.

The Argument That Profit Does Not Belong in the Schools

Profit has been in the schools for a long time. Private firms have built schools, sold schools textbooks, sold schools classroom supplies and engaged in numerous other market transactions for years. All of this has been done at a profit. In a competitive environment, this profit has encouraged firms to provide better and lower-cost services to schools in ways that save money and benefit children. All of this private profit has occurred alongside the decades-long history of privatization of school support services discussed earlier in this primer.

[liv] Note that the question of removing and reassigning the employee will be the contractor's responsibility. The district will not face the complaints that might have been made if a district employee were summarily removed from the workplace under similar circumstances.

[lv] See, for instance, the apparent failure of a Traverse City Area Public Schools bus driver to note that a 3-year-old had fallen asleep on the bus, so that the child was transported to the district garage, rather than the school (Christine Finger, "Mother Has Questions after Son Is Left on Bus," Traverse City Record Eagle, May 31, 2007, http://www.record-eagle.com/2007/may/31kidonbus.htm.); similarly, a Gaylord Community Schools bus driver reportedly made several children leave the bus before their scheduled stop, despite the children's protests that they did not know where they were (Sheri McWhirter, "Driver Forced Students Off Bus, Officials Say," Traverse City Record Eagle, June 11, 2006, http://www.record-eagle.com/2006/jun/11bus.htm.).

The Argument That Privatization Has Failed Elsewhere

Privatization, like any other human enterprise, can fail. Moreover, contracts sometimes "fail" due to the militant opposition of those affected by them.

That some deals may sour, however, does not change the fact that most succeed. In fact, if officials follow basic guidelines of good contracting, they can increase the likelihood their contract will save the district money, improve service provision or both.

The overall success of contracting is borne out by the fact that it is increasing, rather than decreasing, among Michigan school districts. Recall that between 2001 and 2006, the number of Michigan school districts that contracted for food, busing or custodial services appears to have risen, reaching 37.7 percent in 2006 — roughly three in eight. Preliminary survey results suggest that number is likely to increase in 2007.[lvi] Moreover, recall that in the 2006 Mackinac Center survey, 74.5 percent of Michigan school districts that contract for food, bus or custodial services said that contracting had saved them money (20.2 percent were unsure, and only 3.4 percent said they had not saved money). Moreover, 90.9 percent of Michigan's contracting districts said they were satified with the results of their contracting, while just 5.3 percent said they were not. Preliminary results in the 2007 survey indicate similar results.

And finally, despite the MEA's declared opposition to contracting services with nondistrict employees, the MEA itself was discovered to be outsourcing food, custodial, security and mailing services at the union's own headquarters in East Lansing in 1994.[131] Three out of four of those contracts used nonunion labor.[132]

The likely reason for the union's decision to contract with other firms was rational self-interest. It probably saved the union money, improved the service received or added value in some other way. School districts presumably have the right to seek the same benefits on behalf of students and taxpayers.

[lvi]   In addition, Mackinac Center researchers have noticed an apparent increase in nontraditional contracting, such as contracts for substitute teachers, athletic coaches or principals. In this way, too, privatization appears to be advancing as a management tool.

10 Contracting Rules of Thumb

As noted earlier in this primer, well-executed privatization can save money and improve the quality of services. Poorly executed privatization, on the other hand, can do just the opposite.

The previous section covered a number of technical issues that will help ensure that a district that has decided to privatize achieves a good result. But extensive experience in the private and public sectors over recent decades has pointed to broader guidelines for getting privatization right and avoiding common pitfalls.

This section reviews a number of these broader guidelines. While I have tried to include the most relevant and important contracting advice, I would encourage the reader to be open to further information. For example, district officials interested in contracting for school bus services should acquire the National School Transportation Association's "School Transportation Outsourcing Tool Kit," which is the single best "how-to" guide I know of for competitive contracting of school transportation services.[lvii] The kit also has a detailed "Request for Proposal" that should be very useful to the reader. Readers may also wish to consult the embedded links in the Web version of this primer.

The following 10 rules of thumb are by no means the last word in contracting practices, but they do represent a handy list of key points with which to begin the contracting process.

1. Begin at the End.

School officials wishing to competitively contract services in their districts must begin with the end in mind and work backward. Hence, districts contemplating contracting may wish to review the results of similar contracting attempts in other districts (examples are easy to find), noting particular processes and contract details related to the following questions:

- What were the results of the contracting over time (not just in the first year)?

- What were the results after the first year?

[lvii] "The School Transportation Outsourcing Tool Kit," (Springfield, Virginia: National School Transportation Association, 1999).

- Was the contract renewed?

- Were district officials forced to warn the contractor at any time of perceived performance shortcomings?

- Did either the displaced district employees or the union representing them file an unfair labor practice complaint[lviii] against the school board or try to interfere in other ways with the transition?

2. Visit Other Districts.

More than 37 percent of Michigan school districts contract out for at least one of the three major noninstructional services.[133] Out of a sense of collegiality and professional courtesy, many officials in districts that contract a service will be happy to answer questions from their peers in other districts, give facility tours and discuss how their private contractors operate.

During the privatization process, private vendors that have submitted a proposal to a district will typically invite board members and the superintendent on a tour of another building or district where the vendor is already established. Officials should take these tours but remain careful not to rely on them, because a vendor will naturally select only the gems they wish to showcase. Prudence dictates that officials themselves should select schools districts contracting with particular vendors and tour the facilities without the vendor present. Doing so makes it easier to interview a vendor's staff and to talk to students and school personnel about the contractor's performance.

Writing in the April 1998 issue of The American School Board Journal, education experts William Keane and Samuel Flam listed the site visit as one of the top six things district officials can do to reduce opposition:

> "We cannot emphasize enough how important it is to see a privatization experiment with your own eyes. But seeing it is only part of your responsibility. You also need to ask tough questions,

---

[lviii] An unfair labor practice is an act forbidden by labor law, such as the National Labor Relations Act or the Michigan Public Employment Relations Act. Complaints about such practices can be filed against an employer or against a union.

such as: How much money has privatization saved? How many district employees were laid off as a result of privatization? And, how has the quality of the privatized service improved or declined? If you don't get straight answers and concrete examples, you should be concerned."[134]

Keane and Flam have years of experience in Michigan as upper-level district officials and education consultants. They are also the authors of the book "Public Schools Private Enterprise: What You Should Know and Do About Privatization," which makes many useful points about the privatization process not specifically addressed in this primer. I recommend the book as important background reading.[135]

3. Employ a Timeline.

Skillful project managers understand that they face two major constraints in bringing any project to a successful conclusion: time and resources. Project management has practically become a science over the years, and sophisticated tools, such as project management software, have been developed to help managers meet tight budgets and deadlines. Regardless, for most school districts, a pencil and a legal pad will do just as well at the planning stage.

Simply write out the date by which the district would like to reach its final milestone in a particular contracting process. This milestone might be the school board's approval of a deal or the first renewal of the contract. The important thing is to recognize that time is a serious constraint. By starting from the ideal finish date and working backward through a list of the project's milestones, the district's project manager can better determine what needs to be accomplished and when.

The timeline in Graphic 6 is taken from the SPP RFP for custodial services[136] (which can also be viewed from a hyperlink in Appendix 2 of the online version of this primer).[137] The dates I have added to the graphic are meant to indicate how long a district might take to reach each milestone, but because they are based on an actual contracting process in which the district was under time pressure, the intervals shown in the timeline may be shorter than desirable in other bidding and contracting situations. For instance, management consultant Mark A. Walsh, writing in The School Administrator, recommends that new bids for a bus contract be solicited "five to seven months prior to the expiration of the [current school transportation] contract."[138]

In an RFP, a timeline is spelled out by the district for the benefit of potential vendors, but the timeline should also serve as part of the district's project planning.

Graphic 6: Milestones in a Typical School District Contracting Project

Jan. 2	RFP sent to prospective bidders
Jan. 9	Mandatory pre-bid meeting and site visit (specify time)
Jan. 16	Deadline for submitting written requests for clarification and questions
Jan. 31	Deadline for submitting proposals – bid opening (specify time)
Feb. 7	Evaluation of proposals and recommendation
Feb. 10	Interviews
Feb. 17	Announcement of contract award to contractor; bidders notified of decision
March 17	Contract finalized
March 24	Custodial service operations begin in full[139]

Source: School Purchasing Pages RFP for Custodial Services, with dates added

4. Cast a Wide Net.

If the bidding, awarding and monitoring processes are well-executed, competition between vendors seeking a school district's business can drive the price down and the quality up. Generally speaking, experts in the field of competitive contracting recommend that to ensure a sufficient level of competition, at least three vendors be encouraged to compete in a bidding process.

Like competitive contracting itself, this concept is nothing new. In his 1940 tome "Pupil Transportation in the United States," M.C.S. Noble Jr. of the Teachers College at Columbia University published data on the "Relationship Between the Number of Bids Received and the Cost per Pupil per Month" of privatized school transportation.[140] Mr. Noble reported that at the time, more than 63 percent[141] of all school buses in the United States were privately owned. The data in the table from the 1940 study (reproduced in Graphic 7) shows that the greater the number of bids, the lower the ultimate cost of providing the service.

Graphic 7: The Number of Bids and Per Pupil Costs for School Bus Services (Statistics Published in 1940)

Number of Bids Received Per Bus	Cost Per Pupil Per Month
10	$1.67
9	$1.90
6	$2.42
5	$2.56
4	$2.70
3	$2.78
2	$2.85
1	$2.89
0	$2.93

Source: *"Pupil Transportation in the United States," M.C.S. Noble Jr.*

Competition is the key to successful contracting. Indeed, when recommending privatization, I prefer to use the phrase "competitive contracting."

Consider the case of an Upper Peninsula district that retains two buses in-house to ensure competitive pressure on the limited number of private busing vendors willing to work north of the Mackinac Bridge. Randall Van Gasse, superintendent of the Norway-Vulcan Area Schools, reports that his district has been contracting for bus services since the 1940s, but when new routes open up, the vendors must compete with the in-house drivers for the business.[lix] The competition the private vendors face, he notes wryly, "keeps them honest."[142]

Noble's findings and Van Gasse's experience underscore the importance of ensuring that there is robust competition for a district's business. They also drive home that competitive contracting in school districts is a time-tested approach. Indeed, what is intriguing about Noble's book is its demonstration that "past is prologue." Districts today are debating subjects wrestled with more than 60 years ago.

[lix]   Van Gasse also reports that his district contracts out with a third party for a school principal and substitute teachers.

5. Develop RFP Specifications Independently.

A district can certainly look at the specifications in other school districts' contracts, but district officials should ultimately decide on the RFP and contract specifications independently. In particular, they should not consult potential vendors regarding these specifications. It may be tempting to ask a vendor for help given the vendor's expertise and the complexity of the contracting process, but vendor participation in creating specifications is clearly contrary to the district's own best interests.

First, in food contracting, conferring with a vendor on RFP specifications is prohibited by the federal government.[143] Second, there is a good reason for this prohibition, so districts should avoid such practices even when contracting other school support services. The prohibition exists because too many districts (not necessarily in Michigan) have relied on specifications that may have been designed to thwart rather than facilitate competition. Even a contractor with the best of intentions may subtly skew the RFP in ways that limit the number of competitors or deny the district the wide range of bids that are most likely to provide low cost and high quality service.

6. Monitor. Monitor. Monitor.

The competitive contracting job is not over when the initial deal is struck. District officials have a clear duty to ensure that the contractor meets the specifications they have laid out in the RFP and the signed contract. Indeed, the individuals assigned to ensure that the contractor meets the district's needs and contract provisions should be selected while the RFP is being assembled. This will give the eventual contract monitor the opportunity to develop an institutional memory of the particular contracting process, the personalities involved and the responsibilities of each party in the final contract.

It is important that the contract monitor have no conflict of interest. That is, oversight must be conducted by an individual with nothing to lose or gain personally from measuring and reporting on the performance of the contractor. For example, a district cannot fully rely on information about a contractor's performance from an observer who has close friends or relatives who either lost or received their jobs because of privatization.

John Rehfuss, author of the Reason Foundation's "Designing an Effective Bidding and Monitoring System to Minimize Problems in Competitive Contracting," suggests that rather than using a monitor from the school department that originally provided the service, districts consider using "centralized monitors" who work in the contracting office, "usually the purchasing or procurement office."[144] He argues that although these monitors may be less familiar with the operational details of the service, they tend to be very familiar with the contract itself. "Being more removed from the program," Rehfuss observes, "they are more likely to be disinterested, objective monitors and treat contractors more consistently."[145] Rehfuss argues that good centralized monitors ultimately "can become the basis of an experienced cadre of contracting officers" and reduce the "possibility of collusion between [district] program officers and the contractor."[146]

Likewise, contact between the monitor and bidders should be minimized during the bidding process to preclude not just impropriety (such as providing one contractor with exclusive insider information), but also the appearance of impropriety. This same restriction should apply to other district officials as well.

Kenneth P. May, author of the study of contracting in New Jersey, also recommends that a checklist be developed from the specifications of the RFP.[147] The contract would then specify that the checklist be used in evaluating the contractor's performance, and the contract would then detail penalties for repeated poor evaluations.[148]

This approach has merit. A checklist arranged in advance will warn a contractor what level of service must be provided, provide a paper trail in the event that a district needs to penalize a contractor and encourage a monitor to provide a more complete and objective measure of the contractor's performance than the monitor might otherwise be inclined to give.

7. Choose a Point Person.

The district should choose an individual to be the public face and voice of the privatization effort. Likely candidates include the superintendent or a business officer, but whoever is chosen, it must be clear that he or she has the support of the superintendent and board. Opponents of privatization may work to sow disagreement among key decision-makers in an attempt to thwart the contracting process. A united front will be helpful, even if the unity involves no more than a commitment to simply exploring the topic.

The point person should possess a number of characteristics. First, he or she should have a measure of courage. A point person should be able to maintain his or her composure despite midnight phone calls from hostile individuals and repeated name-calling, boos, hisses and guffaws at school board meetings.

Second, he or she should be media savvy. Privatization efforts are controversial, and controversy is a magnet for media coverage. School employee unions are familiar with media campaigns and are practiced at generating media coverage sympathetic to the union position. The point person must not only be familiar with counterarguments to union talking points, but must be adept at extemporaneously distilling these into quotable rejoinders.

Third, the point person should have experience in a high-profile leadership role. For public relations purposes alone, no district should delegate this key role to a person fresh out of college, for example. Yet gray hairs are not enough; a potential point person must be accustomed to executing complex projects despite public and private criticism.

Board members should be careful to defer public discussions to the point person. An agitated board member ad-libbing on unfamiliar details to a reporter could generate hard feelings, bad media, an unfair labor practice complaint and even a recall campaign.

8. Build a Team.

However talented a superintendent or business officer may be, few individuals have the time or skills to single-handedly shepherd a major privatization program, including post-contract monitoring, to a successful completion. While each district's situation is unique, at least three key people — in addition to the school board — should be involved in controversial privatization efforts.

The first person is the superintendent. Even if he or she does not play a role in investigating privatization, reviewing RFPs or selecting a vendor, the superintendent must be kept apprised of the process at every step. The public will look to the superintendent as the first and final arbiter of the decision to privatize, even though the decision is actually the board's prerogative.[ix] This is why the superintendent often makes the ideal point person for privatization. As the top district official, he or she is usually held responsible for well-managed schools.

The second person is the business officer or equivalent, if the district has one. A good business officer is typically a trained accountant. He or she will bring to the table analytical and financial planning skills that are vital to a successful contracting effort, including the ability to understand and even perform a "full-" or "total-cost accounting analysis" that allows district officials to better gauge how much providing a particular service with the district's own resources actually costs. For instance, the district may pay just one utility bill every month, but a good business officer can often estimate accurately what proportion of the total energy use is due to cafeteria operations. Such estimates allow the district to determine the full cost of providing food services in-house, as opposed to contracting the service with a food service management company.

Such estimates and financial expertise can be critical to a contracting process. Indeed, a school board should consider making a school business officer the project manager and even point person for the district's privatization efforts. At the very least, superintendents who have business officers should work closely with them. When a privatization debate is raging, it is often business officers who can marshal a telling fact quickly, because they're routinely elbow-deep in the finances as a part of their job.

The third person to involve in any privatization process is the district's attorney (or attorneys). True, contracting for services is becoming commonplace, and districts can and do adapt other districts' contracts to their own needs. But one can't assume that what has worked in one district with one vendor will spell success in another. A well-written contract that anticipates a district's specific needs can protect against unexpected charges from a vendor or complaints of unfair labor practices from a union. Lawyers cannot anticipate every problem, but they can minimize contracting pitfalls.

Inevitably, a district's board is collectively the most important part of the district's privatization team. If the majority have no desire

---

[ix]   Indeed, school boards may direct a superintendent to pursue a competitive contracting arrangement even if the superintendent does not prefer to privatize. This situation is not ideal, but it is not necessarily fatal, either.

to pursue privatization, then a fine point person, business officer and superintendent will be for naught. Once a decision has been made to explore privatization initiatives, it is imperative for key project personnel to keep the board informed and solicit feedback either through formal meetings or on an individual basis.

Of course, privatization team members and board members should confer within the bounds of the law. Violating the state's Open Meetings Act, which mandates that certain meetings be to open to the public, is illegal and a sure-fire way to cause a self-inflicted wound. That said, superintendents are not prohibited from speaking to board members individually.

One assistant superintendent I recently interviewed said that he will speak to board members individually to solicit any questions or concerns they might have before the board actually meets. He recommends other superintendents do the same when contracting. By discovering in advance what questions board members want to ask at official meetings, a superintendent can be prepared to provide answers. This official says he has also privately helped prepare individual board members for potentially rancorous public reactions to privatization proposals at official meetings.[149]

One last note: One district official who has been part of a contracting team recommends that the school's Freedom of Information Act officer be alerted and kept on hand when the privatization process begins. A series of FOIA inquiries from opponents of privatization is likely to follow.

9. Recommend a Safety Net for Workers.

Districts frequently request in the RFP that potential contractors give first consideration to existing district employees when hiring new people to provide the privatized service. This preference not only benefits the workers, who will naturally be uneasy about the loss of their current jobs, but the company itself. Indeed, most companies are eager to tap the institutional knowledge the current workers will bring with them. In Midland, Chartwells School Dining is actually scheduled to host a job fair for displaced employees and will bus those interested to a nearby district for a tour of a Chartwells-run cafeteria.

At the same time, the district should not mandate that the contractor hire school district personnel. Management flexibility is one of the attributes that allow a private contractor to save money in the first place, and the district will put its cost savings and service quality at risk if it removes the contractor's ability to manage personnel independently.

10. Videotape Public Proceedings.

As mentioned earlier, school board meetings will probably become much more controversial when a district's decision to privatize services becomes public. For legal and strategic reasons, the board should have the meeting videotaped, a recommendation made by Jim Palm, an assistant superintendent for the Berrien County Intermediate School District. As Palm notes, videotaping will create an accurate record of what was said at board meetings, providing clarity in the event a grievance or a lawsuit is filed. A videotape will also enable the board to defend its actions to reporters and the public if questions are raised about school board comments or transactions at the meeting.

Public Involvement in the Privatization Process

There are two schools of thought on the degree to which a superintendent or individual board members should publicize an investigation into privatization. A given district's approach will probably be a judgment call that rests largely on the particular character and circumstances of the community in which the privatization will take place.

In some districts, the investigation might occur best in a public setting, particularly if the move to competitively contract was initially proposed by community members. In Midland, for example, the school district solicited feedback from local citizens on how to improve its operations. Among the ideas recommended was support service privatization. When something like this happens, the discussion will likely become public regardless of the superintendent's or board's preferences.

In other districts, the key proponents of privatization may be district officials who work behind the scenes long before they announce their intentions to contract a particular service. The idea is to develop a clear picture of what privatization might accomplish before a grueling public battle begins. In the Berrien County Intermediate School District, one official quietly issued a formal RFP and received proposals from vendors before the union that represented the area's school transportation employees knew the process had begun. The result was that the ISD board held only two meetings packed with angry employees, their families and friends, instead of nine or 10 meetings, as has been the case elsewhere.

There are advantages and drawbacks to both approaches. The first may allow valuable public debate that improves the privatization process, while the second may avoid riling district employees, their unions and the community over a privatization investigation that shows that the service should remain in-house after all.

Regardless of the approach a district chooses, its very earliest steps should probably be discreet. School district employees, like anyone else in such a situation, will be concerned about their job security and income, even if they are likely to be hired by the winning contractor. Alarming them when the privatization may not take place seems unnecessary.

That said, districts will find that attempts to contact vendors indirectly are self-defeating (and even potentially problematic, given district guidelines and state laws like the Open Meetings Act). District officials, for instance, may be tempted to ask third parties to investigate contracting on their behalf to minimize the possibility that their interest in privatization will be made public. Unfortunately, this approach will also mean that the district go-between will be unable to provide a vendor with specific details for fear of identifying the district. This prevents a vendor from contributing any estimates that might be useful. For instance, if a food-services vendor knows nothing more than that a district has 500 to 1,000 students, the vendor will find it extremely difficult to make a meaningful estimate of what the costs to the district would be if the vendor assumed control.

Conclusion

The landscape of public education in Michigan has changed dramatically over the last 13 years. Most districts receive a majority of their operating money from state government, not local taxes. Charter schools and nearby districts draw students away from local schools and capture the state money that goes with them. Districts are even subject to new reporting and student testing mandates, with the results available in seconds through the Internet from almost anywhere in the nation.

School districts have thus been forced to stand out from their neighbors, particularly through academic quality, the one product everyone expects schools to produce and the one quality everyone tries to quantify. Districts with unexceptional academic results are less likely to attract students, balance budgets and placate legislators.

In this environment, privatization is a simplifier. The day-to-day responsibilities of transporting students, feeding them or keeping their schools clean are delegated to private firms that can be penalized or fired for failure, even as other firms wait to fill the breach. District officials become freer to help teachers with the difficult but central job of academic improvement and discovery.

This does not mean that privatization ends the need to supervise noninstructional services. Contract specifications, bidding procedures, bid evaluations and contract monitoring require time and discipline. But with privatization of major noninstructional services in Michigan now occurring in three school districts in eight, and with most of the contracting districts claiming cost savings and satisfaction, the potential of privatization to liberate district resources for academic pursuits seems clear. Districts that explore contracting may discover not only a better business plan, but a new commitment to their mission as well.

Appendix 1:
A Recent Privatization
Court Challenge

The Three Legal Challenges to Privatization in Grand Rapids
By Patrick J. Wright[lxi]

In 2007, the Michigan Education Association, the state's largest school employees union, scored partial victories in civil and administrative lawsuits involving privatization of school bus services in the Grand Rapids Public Schools. The union's success in the civil lawsuit did not directly affect the school district, however, and depended on facts unique to the case. In addition, the administrative decision may well be overturned.

The lawsuits occurred in the context of a long-term legal strategy by the MEA, a union that is explicitly "committed to defeating privatization."[150] Following passage of Michigan's Public Act 112 of 1994, the union filed a legal challenge to the act's prohibition on the discussion of noninstructional services privatization during the collective bargaining process.[lxii] In 1996, the Michigan Supreme Court denied the MEA's claim that the provision was unconstitutional.[151] The court further stated that even if a school district agreed during collective bargaining never to privatize noninstructional services, the promise would be unenforceable, since privatization is an illegal subject of bargaining.[152]

This broader legal attack having failed, the MEA has brought legal challenges against privatization on a case-by-case basis. The union has used three basic claims: a tort action in state court against the contractor providing the service; a federal claim of unfair labor practices against the contractor for refusing to recognize the MEA as the collective bargaining agent for the private employees providing the service; and a state unfair labor practice claim or contract grievance against a school district alleging repudiation of a collective bargaining agreement.

The MEA used all three claims in its challenge to school bus privatization in the Grand Rapids Public Schools. They are discussed in detail below.

[lxi] Appendix 1 was written by Patrick J. Wright, a senior legal analyst with the Mackinac Center for Public Policy and a former Michigan Supreme Court commissioner and Michigan assistant attorney general.

[lxii] MCL § 423.215(3); MCL § 423.215(3)(f). See the discussion of this law under "School Districts' Administrative Powers: Public Act 112 of 1994," Page 36.

State-Level Tort Action Against the Private Company

The Grand Rapids Educational Support Personnel Association, an affiliate of the MEA, consists of nonteaching, nonclerical employees, including about 168 "bus drivers, mechanics, and 'dispatch/route planners.'"[153] According to court records, GRESPA entered into a collective bargaining agreement with the Grand Rapids school district from July 1, 2004 to June 30, 2006.[154]

In April 2004, two months before the collective bargaining agreement took effect, Dean Management Services obtained a management contract for the district's bus services.[155] GRESPA subsequently claimed that Dean Management induced the school district to privatize the management services by not disclosing all key cost-cutting strategies during its management term and saving those strategies for its later transportation proposal.[156] The union further alleged that on April 15, 2005, Dean Management secretly met with the Grand Rapids school board in violation of the Open Meetings Act and proposed that Dean Transportation, a sister firm, should be hired to provide all transportation services, not merely management, for the Grand Rapids schools.[157] The board, without seeking other bids, informally approved the deal on April 18, 2005.

Almost immediately, the MEA filed suit against Dean Transportation (but not the school district) in state circuit court and alleged "tortious interference" with contract and "tortious interference" with business expectations. Dean, in turn, sought to have the complaint dismissed under the provisions of Public Act 112.

The court denied Dean's motion to dismiss, holding that if Dean Transportation solicited the district while the collective bargaining agreement was in force, the company could be held liable.[158] The court also stipulated, however, that if the company merely accepted the district's offer, no liability would follow.[159]

Following this ruling, Dean Transportation and the district both presented evidence that privatization was the district's idea. Dean then filed a second motion to dismiss, but the court allowed the case to proceed on grounds that sufficient circumstantial evidence existed to the contrary. In particular, the trial court noted, "When preparing its proposal for a management contract, Dean asked for, and got, detailed information pertinent only to a full assumption of transportation services, and Dean's eventual bid for a management contract discussed 'future services' it could also provide."[160] In other words, Dean Management allegedly improperly received information in the course of negotiating a contract for management services that would have unfairly advantaged Dean Transportation in seeking a contract for actual transportation operations.

The parties settled out of court before trial. According to the Mackinac Center's Michigan Education Report, the MEA had requested $30 million, and Dean Transportation agreed to pay $600,000, calling the settlement a "business decision."[161]

In sum, this case appears to have been highly dependent on unique facts. In most cases, no suit against the private company will be possible, since the district will have clearly and publicly initiated the contact with any potential vendors. In the Dean lawsuit, the trial judge appears to have relied on the unique facts related to Dean's previous management contract to allow the suit to proceed.

Dean might have had some strong issues on appeal, but given the risk of a large jury award and the cost of litigation, Dean's decision to settle was probably pragmatic. In any event, the case demonstrates that whatever the risk to the private company in a privatization, the fear of a tort suit against the school district itself should probably not be a factor in a district's decision to privatize.

Federal Unfair Labor Practice: the "Successorship Doctrine"

Another risk that falls primarily on the private contractor is that the union will claim the automatic privilege to represent workers hired from the school district by the private contractor if those employees work in the same or a similar job. In such instances, the union effectively claims the right to move to the private company along with the employees.

The alleged basis of this argument is known as the "successorship doctrine," a concept the U.S. Supreme Court has endorsed in cases involving the movement of employees from one private firm to another. In particular, the court has upheld the doctrine when, "The new employer makes a conscious decision to maintain generally the same business and to hire a majority of its employees from the predecessor."[162] The courts look for a "substantial continuity" between the employers, considering such factors as "whether the business of both employers is essentially the same; whether the employees of the new company are doing the same jobs in the same working conditions under the same supervisors; and whether the new entity has the same production process, produces the same products, and basically has the same body of customers."[163] This analysis is performed from the employees' perspective.[164] Where such "successorship" is found, the union retains the right to collectively bargain on behalf of the employees. (The new employer, however, is not typically bound by the terms of the union's collective bargaining agreement with the old employer.[165])

In the case of Dean Transportation, GRESPA filed a claim of an unfair labor practice on grounds that Dean refused to recognize GRESPA as the collective bargaining agent of those Dean employees that had formerly worked for the district. In a ruling by an administrative judge of the National Labor Relations Board, GRESPA's claim was upheld. The judge ruled that since Dean Transportation hired a sufficient number of former district bus drivers, GRESPA still represented those workers.

This ruling is currently being reviewed by the NLRB. If affirmed, this ruling could negatively affect privatization efforts, since many private employers would not want to inherit a union.

Regardless, there are good reasons to believe that this ruling will be overturned on appeal to the federal courts. The Supreme Court has not sanctioned the use of the successorship doctrine when the former employer is a public employer and the new employer is a private employer. In fact, the court has noted that there are significant differences between public-sector unionism and private-sector unionism. Public-sector employers often have no competition for the service provided and thus lack the "important discipline" of market pressure.[166] Public-sector employees help decide the public-sector managers with whom they negotiate through their right to vote in school board elections.[167] In addition, many states, including Michigan, prohibit public-sector unions from striking,[168] while any private-sector union covered by the National Labor Relations Act has the legal right to strike.[lxiii] [169]

Hence, joining a public-sector union entails less risk than joining a private-sector union. As noted above, many public-sector unions lack the ability to strike and avoid the subsequent risks of doing so. In addition, public-sector employees are largely immune to market

---

[lxiii] The National Labor Relations Act covers nearly all private-sector unions not involved in the railway or airline industries.

pressures, meaning the risk that a generous union contract will price government workers out of their jobs is much less immediate. The risk of displacement can be further reduced by union power in the political realm.

In contrast, private-sector unions pose more risks for workers. Private-sector unions can strike, and they can also be locked out. If they raise labor costs so high that an employer is no longer competitive in the marketplace, workers can lose their jobs.

Given the lesser risk in public-sector unionism, it's not surprising that 2006 figures from the U.S. Bureau of Labor Statistics show that the nationwide union membership rate is 7.4 percent for private-sector workers, but 36.2 percent for public-sector workers — nearly five times as high.[170] Aside from the distinctions detailed above, this gap alone suggests that many of those willing to join a union in the public sector might not join one in the private sector, particularly when a new right to strike is involved.

Federal courts therefore can (and should) find legal grounds for refusing to apply the successorship doctrine to Dean Transportation and GRESPA. GRESPA's original certification as a union by Grand Rapids school district employees involved the understanding that the union could not legally strike and that Grand Rapids employees could not be legally locked out. Since GRESPA would have such powers and run such risks acting as a union at Dean Transportation, a court would have substantial grounds for concluding that GRESPA must first go through private-sector union certification process — usually a new certification vote by the employees — before representing any employees at Dean Transportation.

The NLRB administrative law judge did not address the union's power to strike or similar issues in his decision that the successorship doctrine applied to the instant case. His decision is being appealed both on the technical application of the successorship doctrine and on the broad issue of whether the doctrine should ever apply where the union originally lacked the ability to strike under state law. The broad issue has never been addressed by the NLRB or the federal courts, so this case may eventually serve as a national precedent.

State Unfair Labor Practice Charge or Contract Grievance:
Repudiation of Collective Bargaining Agreement

The third manner in which the MEA can challenge privatization in the legal arena is to file an unfair labor practice charge or a contract grievance alleging that the district's decision to privatize repudiates the collective bargaining agreement. This allegation would be based on a particular reading of the language of Public Act 112:

> "Collective bargaining between a public school employer and a bargaining representative of its employees shall not include . . . [t]he decision of whether or not to contract with a third party for 1 or more noninstructional support services; or the procedures for obtaining the contract; or the identity of the third party; or the impact of the contract on individual employees or the bargaining unit."[lxiv]

This language can be viewed as allowing a district to privatize noninstructional services, but not empowering it to do so in the middle of a collective bargaining agreement. The MEA has in fact used this argument to file unfair labor practice claims and contract grievances for arbitration.

Significantly, however, in no case has the MEA allowed the issue to be decided by a court of law or an administrative law judge at the Michigan Employment Relations Commission. In the case of Grand Rapids and Dean Transportation,[171] GRESPA withdrew its charge before there was a hearing.

The union challenged an Albion Public Schools privatization decision along similar lines. In this case, an administrative law judge held a hearing and informed the MEA that she would rule against it.[172] The MEA quickly withdrew its unfair labor practice charges.[173] And in the case of the Hartland Community Schools' custodial privatization, the union settled for $20,000,[174] a sum small enough that the district may have reasoned that settling was cheaper than the legal cost of fighting the charge.

The union's voluntary withdrawal of its unfair labor practice claims in the Albion and Grand Rapids disputes suggest that it sees a definitive

---

[lxiv] See endnote 86.

decision interpreting the privatization provision of Public Act 112 as contrary to its interests. Nevertheless, the MEA's past actions are no guarantee that the union will not fully pursue a similar unfair labor practice charge in the future. Given the costly relief the MEA would seek if it were to prevail — reinstatement of the former or privatized employees — a decision to privatize is not entirely free of legal risk. And as the Hartland case suggests, as long as the general threat of such grievances is still viable, the union can raise the bar to privatization by extracting relatively small amounts from districts that lack the resources to pay for a long legal battle. The MEA's coffers dwarf those of many of Michigan school districts.

Moreover, the union can file a separate contract grievance arguing that the board has violated the collective bargaining agreement by privatizing the service. GRESPA has in fact filed a grievance against the Grand Rapids Public Schools alleging such a breach. The grievance was summarily denied by an arbitrator, but the trial judge vacated this ruling on procedural (not substantive) grounds and ordered a new hearing. This arbitration hearing is pending at the time of publication of this primer.

Such grievances and legal challenges will end only when there is a definitive ruling from the state courts that privatizing in the middle of a collective bargaining agreement is (or is not) permissible. On balance, however this threat to any particular district appears to be modest.

Summary

School districts that are considering privatization should consult with their attorneys to discuss legal issues. The easiest time to privatize is at the end of a collective bargaining agreement. Contracting for noninstructional services during a collective bargaining agreement may be permissible under Public Act 112 of 1994, but this approach entails a risk that the union might fully pursue and prevail in an unfair labor practice complaint or contract grievance alleging repudiation of a collective bargaining agreement.

On the tort front, most of the legal risk — to the extent a risk exists — falls on the private vendor. As long as the district approaches the private companies, however, tort suits can probably be avoided. In addition, there is a good chance that either the National Labor Relations

Board or the federal courts will hold that the successorship doctrine does not apply when a public-sector union that lacked the power to strike seeks to continue representing employees that have entered the private sector.

To sum up, with appropriate legal help, privatization may be proper at any time.

Appendix 2:
Sample RFPs, Company Responses and Contracts

Below are Web addresses for key documents produced during the contracting process in a variety of Michigan school districts.[lxv] These are provided as a reference source for readers interested in the details of the contracting process. Readers should note, however, that some of the documents are better examples of contracting than others.

Custodial

Atherton Community Schools — Request for Proposal, Part 1:
http://www.mackinac.org/archives/2007/rfp/cust/Atherton-RFP.pdf

Atherton Community Schools — RFP, Part 2:
http://www.mackinac.org/archives/2007/rfp/cust/Atherton-RFP%20part%202.pdf

Atherton Community Schools — Company Response:
http://www.mackinac.org/archives/2007/rfp/cust/Atherton-Company%20response.pdf

Atlanta Community Schools — Company Response:
http://www.mackinac.org/archives/2007/rfp/cust/Atlanta-Company%20response.pdf

Bellaire Public Schools — Contract:
http://www.mackinac.org/archives/2007/rfp/cust/Bellaire-Contract.pdf

Gobles Public Schools — RFP:
http://www.mackinac.org/archives/2007/rfp/cust/Gobles-RFP.pdf

Gobles Public Schools — Company Response:
http://www.mackinac.org/archives/2007/rfp/cust/Gobles-Company%20response.pdf

Gobles Public Schools — Company Response Summary:
http://www.mackinac.org/archives/2007/rfp/cust/
Gobles-Company%20response%20summary.pdf

Jackson Public Schools — RFP:
http://www.mackinac.org/archives/2007/rfp/cust/Jackson-RFP.pdf

Jackson Public Schools — Contract:
http://www.mackinac.org/archives/2007/rfp/cust/Jackson-Contract.pdf

Midland Public Schools — RFP:
http://www.mackinac.org/archives/2007/rfp/cust/MPS-RFP.pdf

Midland Public Schools — Additional Specifications:
http://www.mackinac.org/archives/2007/rfp/cust/MPS-RFP Additional Specifications.pdf

Pentwater Public Schools — RFP:
http://www.mackinac.org/archives/2007/rfp/cust/Pentwater-RFP.pdf

---

[lxv] The Web addresses are live hyperlinks in the online HTML version of this primer.

Food

Clawson Public Schools — Contract:
http://www.mackinac.org/archives/2007/rfp/food/Clawson-Contract.pdf

Croswell-Lexington Schools — RFP:
http://www.mackinac.org/archives/2007/rfp/food/Croswell-Lexington-RFP.pdf

Croswell-Lexington Schools — Contract:
http://www.mackinac.org/archives/2007/rfp/food/Croswell-Lexington-Contract.pdf

East China School District — RFP:
http://www.mackinac.org/archives/2007/rfp/food/East%20China-RFP.pdf

East China School District — Contract:
http://www.mackinac.org/archives/2007/rfp/food/East%20China-Contract.pdf

Gobles Public Schools — Contract:
http://www.mackinac.org/archives/2007/rfp/food/Gobles-Contract.pdf

Grosse Pointe Public Schools — Contract Amendment:
*http://www.mackinac.org/archives/2007/rfp/food/Grosse%20Pointe-
Contract%20Amendment.pdf*

Houghton Lake Community Schools — Contract:
http://www.mackinac.org/archives/2007/rfp/food/Houghton%20Lake-Contract.pdf

Jackson Public Schools — RFP:
http://www.mackinac.org/archives/2007/rfp/food/Jackson-RFP.pdf

Jackson Public Schools — Contract:
http://www.mackinac.org/archives/2007/rfp/food/Jackson-Contract.pdf

Marcellus Community Schools — Contract:
http://www.mackinac.org/archives/2007/rfp/food/Marcellus-Contract.pdf

Monroe Public Schools — RFP, Part 1:
http://www.mackinac.org/archives/2007/rfp/food/Monroe-RFP%20part%201.pdf

Monroe Public Schools — RFP, Part 2:
http://www.mackinac.org/archives/2007/rfp/food/Monroe-RFP%20part%202.pdf

Monroe Public Schools — RFP, Part 3:
http://www.mackinac.org/archives/2007/rfp/food/Monroe-RFP%20part%203.pdf

Monroe Public Schools — Contract:
http://www.mackinac.org/archives/2007/rfp/food/Monroe-Contract.pdf

New Haven Community Schools — RFP:
http://www.mackinac.org/archives/2007/rfp/food/New%20Haven-RFP.pdf

New Haven Community Schools — Contract:
http://www.mackinac.org/archives/2007/rfp/food/New%20Haven-Contract.pdf

River Rouge School District — Contract:
http://www.mackinac.org/archives/2007/rfp/food/River%20Rouge-Contract.pdf

State of Michigan Prototype — RFP and Instructions:[lxvi]
http://www.mackinac.org/archives/2007/rfp/food/State prototype RFP.doc

State of Michigan Prototype — Worksheets:
http://www.mackinac.org/archives/2007/rfp/food/State prototype worksheets.xls

U.S. Department of Agriculture Web Site With Food
and Nutrition Service Governance Memos:
http://www.fns.usda.gov/cnd/Governance/policy.htm

Whittemore-Prescott Area Schools — RFP:
http://www.mackinac.org/archives/2007/rfp/food/Whittemore-Prescott-RFP.pdf

Whittemore-Prescott Area Schools — Contract:
http://www.mackinac.org/archives/2007/rfp/food/Whittemore-Prescott-Contract.pdf

Transportation

Tecumseh Public Schools — RFP:
http://www.mackinac.org/archives/2007/rfp/trans/Tecumseh-RFP.pdf

Tecumseh Public Schools — Contract:
http://www.mackinac.org/archives/2007/rfp/trans/Tecumseh-Contract.pdf

---

[lxvi] The state of Michigan documents listed here should be used for reference only. Readers interested in obtaining a sample food-service contract should contact the state directly, since the contracts and instructions for food-service contracting are updated regularly in accordance with changes in state and federal regulations.

Appendix 3:
Contractors Operating in Michigan School Districts

Appearing below are vendors that had contracts with Michigan's conventional school districts in 2006. The list is complete with the exception of a few contractors for which no contact information could be found.

This list is provided for informational purposes only. A company's presence on the list in no way implies an endorsement of that company by the author or the Mackinac Center for Public Policy.

Food Service

Chartwells School Dining
3600 Camelot DR. SE, Suite 3
Grand Rapids, MI 49546
(989) 366-4411

Taher, Inc.
5570 Smetana Drive
Minnetonka, MN 55343
(952) 945-0505

Aramark School Support Services
45399 William Court
Canton, MI 48188
(734) 748-0639

Sodexho School Services
3020 Woodcreek Dr. Suite B
Downers Grove, IL 60515
(317) 769-5535

Arbor Management Inc.
2100 Corporate Drive, Suite B
Addison, IL 60101-5134
(630) 620-5134

Consolidated Vendors Corporation
48129 West Road
Wixom, MI 48393
(248) 347-2429

Continental Dining
and Refreshment Services
448000 North I-94 Service Drive
Belleville, MI 48111
(734) 699-4100

Creative Dining Services
1 Royal Park Drive, Suite #3
Zeeland, MI 49464
(616) 748-1700

Gourmet Services, Inc.
82 Piedmont Avenue
Atlanta, GA 30303
(404) 876-5700

Kosch Catering and
Corporate Dining
324 East Street
Rochester, MI 48307
(248) 608-0690 x-18

Nutritional Management Services
2361 Main Street
London, ON N6P1A7
CANADA
(519) 652-2800

Ovations Dining Services
PO Box 261
New Hudson, MI 48165

Preferred Meal Systems, Inc.
3050 Union Lake Road, Suite 8F
Commerce, MI 48382
(248) 360-0928

Custodial Services

Grand Rapids Building Services
1200 Front Avenue
Grand Rapids, MI 49504
(616) 451-2064

Hi-Tec Building Services
6578 Roger Drive
Jenison, MI 49428
(616) 662-1623

Enviro-Clean
3801 Eastern Avenue SE
Grand Rapids, MI 49508-2414

At Your Service
3711 Gorey Avenue
Flint, MI 48506
(810) 715-1100

CSM Services
3536 Highland Dr.
Hudsonville, MI 49426-1909
(616) 667-0037

DM Burr Facilities Management
4126 Holiday Drive
Flint, MI 48507
(888) 533-4600

Knight Facilities Management
304 S Niagara Street
Saginaw, MI 48602
(989) 793-8820

Great Lakes Cleaning Service
216 Court Street
St. Joseph, MI 49085
(269) 983-3050

All In One Cleaning
202 Center Street
Douglas, MI 49406
(269) 857-4222

Jani-King
27777 Franklin Road, Suite 900
Southfield, MI 48034
(248) 936-0040

SCI
PO Box 339
2672 US Highway 41
Marquette, MI 49855
(906) 226-2612

Greater Flint Janitorial
PO Box 1
Davison, MI 48423
(810) 715-8300

UP Janitorial Service
47750 Old Mill Hill Road
Atlantic Mine, MI 49905-9708
(906) 482-3053

D&L Janitorial Service
47420 State Highway M26
Houghton, MI 49931-2819
(906) 482-3873

Spiffy Clean
40 Grimes Road
Negaunee, MI 49866
(906) 475-5611

D&D Maintenance
1003 Industrial Boulevard
Albion, MI 49224
(517) 629-2173

Pro-Klean, Inc.
301 E Breitung Avenue
Kingsford, MI 49802
(906) 774-9466

West Michigan Janitorial
5160 West River Drive NE
Comstock, MI 49321
(616) 647-0552

Northern Floorcare
1538 N Schoenherr Road
Custer, MI 49405
(231) 757-9743

Gett's Cleaning Service
19525 W Old U 2
Watersmeet, MI 49969
(906) 358-3076

Transportation

Triumph Transportation
3718 High Street
Ecorse, MI 48229-1662
(313) 381-5881

Trinity Transportation
1100 Biddle Avenue
Wyandotte, MI 48192
(734) 284-9229

Laidlaw Education Services
55 Shuman Boulevard
Naperville, IL 60563
(630) 848-3000

Dean Transportation
4726 Aurelius Road
Lansing, MI 48910-5805

Rochon Buses
1247 Curry Road
Norway, MI 49870-2227
(906) 563-9496

Lar-El
800 State Street
Kingsford, MI 49802
(906) 774-0696

Marysville School Bus
1421 Michigan Avenue
Marysville, MI 48040
(810) 364-7789

Pellegrini Buses
N1241 River Road
Vulcan, MI 49892

Superior Coaches
2455 Brinkhaus Circle
Chaska, MN 55318
(952) 368-9251

Schilleman's Bus Service
118 Airport Road
Eagle River, WI 54521

First Student
705 Central Avenue, Suite 300
Cincinnati, OH 45202
(513) 241-2200

Endnotes

1   E.S. Savas, "Privatization: Past, Present, Future," in *Annual Privatization Report 2006: Transforming Government through Privatization*, ed. Leonard C. Gilroy (Los Angeles: Reason Foundation, 2006), 3, 24.

2   "Largest Federal Divestiture Completed, Elk Hills Transferred to Private Owner," ed. United States Department of Energy (February 5, 1998), 170.

3   "Federal Update," in *Annual Privatization Report 2006: Transforming Government through Privatization*, ed. Leonard C. Gilroy (Reason Foundation, 2006), 47-54.

4   "Annual Privatization Report 2006: Transforming Government through Privatization," ed. Leonard C. Gilroy (Los Angeles: Reason Foundation, 2006), 51.

5   "Federal Outsourcing in Michigan," in *Michigan Privatization Report* (2005), 14-15.

6   "Federal Update," 47.

7   "Privatized Accident Fund Celebrates Fifth Anniversary," in *Michigan Privatization Report* (1999), 17.

8   "Bureau of Justice Statistics Bulletin: Prisoners in 2005," ed. United States Department of Justice (2006), 6.

9   E.S. Savas, *Privatization in the City: Successes, Failures, Lessons* (Washington, D.C.: CQ Press, 2005).

10 Lei Zhou et al., "Revenues and Expenditures for Public Elementary and Secondary Education: School Year 2004-2005 (Fiscal Year 2005)," (National Center for Education Statistics, U.S. Department of Education, 2007), 2.

11 Brian Maka, e-mail correspondence with Michael LaFaive, May 9, 2007.

12 Ibid.

13 Jack Donahue, *The Warping of Government Work* (Cambridge, Mass.: Harvard University Press, forthcoming).

14 Ibid.

15 ———, e-mail correspondence with Michael LaFaive, May 3, 2007.

16 Author's calculation based on "Registry of Educational Personnel Full-Time Equivalency Data State Level 2005-2006 School Year," (Michigan Center for Educational Performance and Information, 2007).

17 Jay Wortley and Katherine Summers-Coty, "Consensus Revenue Estimates for FY 2006-07 and FY 2007-08 and School Aid Foundation Allowance Index Estimate for Fy 2007-08," (Michigan Senate Fiscal Agency, 2007), 3.

18 Michael D. LaFaive and Ben Stafford, "Survey 2006: School Outsourcing Continues to Grow," (Mackinac Center for Public Policy, 2006), "Table 85, Number of Regular Public School Districts, by Enrollment Size of District: Selected Years, 1990-91 through 2003-04," (National Center for Education Statistics, U.S. Department of Education, 2005).

19 *Section 1990 of Part VII of the Education of Children with Exceptionalities Act, Louisiana State Legislature, Act No. 35 of 2005*, Extraordinary Session 2005.

20 Ibid.

21 Kenneth P. May, "An Investigation into the Role of the Privatization of Non-Instructional Services Provided by New Jersey Public School Districts" (Ed.D. diss., Seton Hall, 1998), 53.

22 Daniel Himebaugh, "Preliminary Brief on Arizona Survey" (research memorandum, Reason Foundation, May 10, 2007). See also Matthew Piccolo, "Preliminary Brief on Florida Survey: Contracting School Services" (research memorandum, Reason Foundation, May 4, 2007).

23 "Dollars & Cents: How Outsourcing Can Save Money for Alabama Schools," (Alabama Policy Institute, 2002), 9.

24 LaFaive and Stafford, "Survey 2006: School Outsourcing Continues to Grow."

25 Howell Wechsler et al., "Food Service and Foods and Beverages Available at School: Results from the School Health Policies and Programs Study 2000," *Journal of School Health* 71, no. 7 (2001): 319.

26 Howell Wechsler, e-mail correspondence with Michael LaFaive, April 19, 2007.

27 May, "An Investigation into the Role of the Privatization of Non-Instructional Services Provided by New Jersey Public School Districts" (diss.), 59.

28 "School Lunch Program: Role and Impacts of Private Food Service Companies," 5.

29 "Subcontracting in the Public Schools Update 2002," 24.

30 "School Lunch Program: Role and Impacts of Private Food Service Companies," 5.

31 "Compass Group: Our Company," http://www.compass-group.com/OurCompany/default.htm.

32 Ernest Farmer, *Accent on Safety: A History of the National Conferences on School Transportation 1939-85* (Tennessee Department of Education, 1990).

33 Robin Leeds, e-mail correspondence with Michael LaFaive, May 2, 2007.

34 Leeds.

35 "Resources," Connecticut School Transportation Association, http://www.ctschoolbus.org/resources.htm.

36 Leeds.

37 Ibid.

38 Joe Agron, "Keeping It Close to Home," (American School & University, 2001), 28.

39 May, "An Investigation into the Role of the Privatization of Non-Instructional Services Provided by New Jersey Public School Districts" (diss.), 57.

40 "Dollars & Cents: How Outsourcing Can Save Money for Alabama Schools," 9.

41 LaFaive and Stafford, "Survey 2006: School Outsourcing Continues to Grow."

42 Bruce Hutchinson and Leila Pratt, "The Comparative Cost of Privatized Public School Transportation in Tennessee," *Policy Studies Journal* 27, no. 3 (1999).

43 Ibid.: 1.

44 Ibid.

45 Ibid.

46 Bruce Hutchinson and Leila Pratt, "The Comparative Cost of Public School Transportation in Louisiana," (2006).

47 Thomas McMahon, "The Big Get Bigger," *School Bus Fleet*, June/July 2006, 45.

48 Steve Hirano, e-mail correspondence with Michael LaFaive, May 3, 2007.

49 Ibid.Telephone conversation with April 30.

50 Ibid.

51 Ibid.

52 Leeds.

53 McMahon, "The Big Get Bigger."

54 "Laidlaw Education Services," http://www.laidlawschoolbus.com/.
55 "Laidlaw Education Services."
56 Sherri Rodeheffer, telephone conversation with Michael LaFaive, May 2, 2007.
57 Agron, "Keeping It Close to Home," 28.
58 LaFaive and Stafford, "Survey 2006: School Outsourcing Continues to Grow."
59 Barry D. Yost, "Privatization of Educational Services by Contractual Agreement in Virginia Public Schools," (Ed.D. diss., Virginia Polytechnic University, 2000), ii.
60 Ibid., 59.
61 Himebaugh, "Preliminary Brief on Arizona Survey."
62 Piccolo, "Preliminary Brief on Florida Survey: Contracting School Services."
63 "About BSCAI," Building Service Contractors Association International http://www.bscai.org/about/default.asp.
64 LaFaive and Stafford, "Survey 2006: School Outsourcing Continues to Grow."
65 Ibid.
66 Janet Beales, "Doing More With Less: Competitive Contracting for School Support Services," (Reason Foundation, 1994).
67 James Quinn and Frederick Hilmer, "Strategic Outsourcing," *Sloan Management Review* (1994).
68 Kirsten Lundberg, "Private Food Service in Houston's Public Schools? Rod Paige's School-Reform Campaign and the Outsourcing Controversy," (Cambridge: John F. Kennedy School of Government, 2001).
69 ———, "Private Food Service in Houston's Public Schools: Epilogue," (Cambridge: John F. Kennedy School of Government, 2001).
70 Ibid.
71 Michigan Education Report, "DPS Enrollment Down by Thousands," in *Michigan Education Report* (Mackinac Center for Public Policy, 2007).
72 MCL § 388.1705.
73 MCL § 388.1705c.
74 Report, "DPS Enrollment Down by Thousands."
75 Michael Hicks and Michael LaFaive, "Demography Is Destiny," (Mackinac Center for Public Policy, 2006).
76 Ibid.
77 Ibid.
78 "Michigan Job Loss Streak Is Longest since Great Depression," (Ann Arbor: University of Michigan News Service, 2006).
79 Ibid.
80 Wortley and Summers-Coty, "Consensus Revenue Estimates for Fy 2006-07 and Fy 2007-08 and School Aid Foundation Allowance Index Estimate for Fy 2007-08," 3.
81 Ibid.
82 Kirk Sanderson, "Revenue Changes and Retirement Costs in the Public School Employees' Retirement System," (Michigan Senate Fiscal Agency, 2006), 2.
83 Ibid., 6.
84 "Financing Michigan Retired Teacher Pension and Health Care Benefits," (Citizens Research Council of Michigan, 2004), 8.
85 MCL § 423.211.

86	MCL § 423.215(3); MCL § 423.215(3)(f).

87	John A. Bourbeau, "Has Outsourcing/Contracting out Saved Money and/or Improved Service Quality? A Vote Counting-Analysis," (diss., Virginia Polytechnic Institute and State University, 2004).

88	LaFaive and Stafford, "Survey 2006: School Outsourcing Continues to Grow."

89	Brandon Hall, "How to Develop Your Request for Proposal," (Brandon Hall Research, 2002).

90	Ibid.

91	Amy J. Christman, correspondence with parties interested in submitting proposals to Gobles Public Schools for cleaning services, May 25, 2005.

92	Ibid.

93	Samuel and Keane Flam, William, *Public Schools Private Enterprise: What You Should Know and Do About Privatization* (Lanham, MD: Scarecrow Press, 2002), 109-10.

94	"School Purchasing Pages Custodial RFP," (School Purchasing Pages, 2007), 11.

95	"Agreement to Provide Student Transportation Services," (Tecumseh: Tecumseh Public Schools, 2006).

96	Janet Beales, "Doing More With Less: Competitive Contracting for School Support Services," (1994), 14.

97	Angela E. Lackey, "MPS Cuts Run Deep: Custodian, Food Service and Teaching Jobs Affected by Action," *Midland Daily News*, May 15 2007.

98	"School Purchasing Pages Custodial RFP."

99	"School Purchasing Pages Transportation RFP," (School Purchasing Pages, 2007), 2.

100	"School Purchasing Pages Custodial RFP," 11.

101	Ibid., 12.

102	Ibid.

103	Ibid., 15.

104	Ibid.

105	Ibid., 18.

106	"RFP/IFB Prototype Contracts," (Lansing: State of Michigan, Department of Education, 2006).

107	Ibid.

108	Cheryl Schubel, E-mail with James Hohman, November 8, 2006.

109	Ibid.

110	Ibid.

111	Ibid.

112	"School Meals Policy Memos," United States Department of Agriculture, Food and Nutrition Services, http://www.fns.usda.gov/cnd/Governance/policy.htm.

113	Matthew Brouillette and Elizabeth Moser, "School Board President Recounts Struggle to Increase Classroom Spending," (Michigan Education Report, 2001).

114	Ibid.

115	Ibid.

116	Ibid.

117	Ibid.

118 *Beat Privatization: A Step by Step Crisis Action Plan,* (National Education Association, n.d.).

119 Ibid., 3-9.

120 Ibid., 21.

121 Ibid., 22.

122 "Schools for Sale: The Privatization of Non-Instructional School Services " (American Federation of State, County and Municipal Employees, No Date Given).

123 "Standing Strong against Privatization," *MEA Voice* 84, no. 3 (2007).

124 Michael LaFaive, "Setting the Privatization Record Straight," (Mackinac Center for Public Policy, 1999).

125 "MEA: Helping or Hurting Education?," http://www.mackinac.org/mea/ii.htm.

126 Ibid.

127 Ibid.

128 Ibid.

129 Ibid.

130 "School Purchasing Pages Transportation RFP," 15.

131 "MEA: Helping or Hurting Education?."

132 Ibid.

133 LaFaive and Stafford, "Survey 2006: School Outsourcing Continues to Grow."

134 Samuel Flam and William Keane, "Politics and Privatization," *American School Board Journal* 185, no. 4 (1998): 48.

135 Flam, *Public Schools Private Enterprise: What You Should Know and Do About Privatization.*

136 "School Purchasing Pages Custodial RFP," 8.

137 See http://www.mackinac.org/8640.

138 Mark A. Walsh, "Managing Your District's Bus Contractor," *The School Administrator,* June 2002, 33.

139 "School Purchasing Pages Custodial RFP."

140 Noble, *Pupil Transportation in the United States,* 215.

141 Ibid.

142 Randy Van Gasse, telephone conversation with Michael LaFaive, May 18, 2007.

143 Stanley Garnett, "School Districts and Federal Procurement Regulations," (Food and Nutrition Service, U.S. Department of Agriculture, 2006), 1, http://www.fns .usda.gov/cnd/Governance/Policy-Memos/2006/2006-03-16.pdf, (accessed June 5, 2007).

144 John Rehfuss, "Designing an Effective Bidding and Monitoring System to Minimize Problems in Competitive Contracting," (Los Angeles and Midland: Reason Foundation and Mackinac Center for Public Policy, 1994).

145 Ibid.

146 Ibid.

147 Kenneth P. May, e-mail correspondence with Michael LaFaive, May 31, 2007.

148 Ibid.

149 Jim Palm, telephone conversation with Michael LaFaive, May 18, 2007.

150 "MEA Committed to Defeating Privatization," *MEA Voice* 84, no. 3 (2007), 2.

151 *Michigan State AFL-CIO v Employment Relations Comm'n*, 453 Mich 362, 379-82 (1996).
152 Ibid., 380, n. 9.
153 *Dean Transp, Inc*, Nos. GR 7-CA-49003 and GR 7-CB-15014, September 27, 2006 Decision, 4-5.
154 Ibid., *4*.
155 *Grand Rapids Educ Support Pers Ass'n v Dean Transp, Inc*, No. 05-04837-CZ Order of December 30, 2005, 2.
156 Ibid., 13.
157 Ibid., 2.
158 Ibid., *12*.
159 Ibid.
160 *Grand Rapids Educ Support Pers Ass'n v Dean Transp, Inc*, No. 05-04837 Order of July 26, 2006 at 5.
161 "Dean Transportation, MEA at Odds over Unions: Bus Company to Appeal Ruling," *Michigan Education Report*, February 23, 2007, 12, http://www.educationreport.org/pubs/mer/article.asp?ID=8243 (accessed June 11, 2007).
162 *Fall River Dyeing & Finishing Corp v NLRB*, 482 US 27, 41 (1987).
163 Ibid., 43.
164 Ibid.
165 Ibid., 40.
166 *Abood v. Detroit Bd. of Educ.*, 431 US 209, 228 (1977).
167 Ibid.
168 Ibid., 229; MCL § 423.202.
169 29 U.S.C. § 163.
170 "Union Members in 2006," (U.S. Department of Labor: Bureau of Labor Statistics, 2007), 8, http://www.bls.gov/news.release/pdf/union2.pdf, (accessed June 11, 2007).
172 Ruthanne Okun, director of the Michigan Employment Relations Commission, phone conversation with Patrick J. Wright, May 2007.
173 *Albion Public Schools*, C06 J-246, Order of May 3, 2007.
174 *Hartland Consolidated Schools*, Case No. C06 F-146, February 2, 2007 Settlement Agreement.

INDEX